Indelible Mark

Indelible Mark

José Octavio Velasco-Tejeda

Library of Congress Control Number: 2015901234
ISBN: Hardcover   978-1-4633-9931-3
                 Softcover   978-1-4633-9930-6
                 eBook   978-1-4633-9929-0

Print information available on the last page.

Rev. date: 28/05/2015

To order additional copies of this book, please contact:
Palibrio
1663 Liberty Drive
Suite 200
Bloomington, IN 47403
Toll Free from the U.S.A 877.407.5847
Toll Free from Mexico 01.800.288.2243
Toll Free from Spain 900.866.949
From other International locations +1.812.671.9757
Fax: 01.812.355.1576
orders@palibrio.com
701283

CONTENTS

CHRISTOPHER ERIC HITCHENS

Christopher Eric Hitchens (13 April 1949 – 15 December 2011), was an English writer, resident of the U.S. He graduated in Philosophy, and Political Sciences and Economy at Balliol College in Oxford. To me, his best book was *God is not Great*. His capacity and ability to debate and to make slivers of his adversaries who were completely unable to respond to the questions or statements were enormous. What courage of these guys, knowing that they had not the slightest chance!

BOOKS WRITTEN IN ENGLISH BY THE SAME AUTHOR

(soon available in Spanish)

Deluxe chimp
Indelible Mark

Book written in Spanish by the same author
(soon available in English):

Anécdotas, Aventuras, Relatos y Conceptos Interesantes

(Anecdotes, Adventures, Stories and Interesting Concepts)

Science fiction novel written in English by the
same author (soon available in Spanish):

Do you want to live, or pass?
(Quires vivir, o ¿pasas?)

S parse throughout this book there appear upper case phrases enclosed by parenthesis, such as: (10 QUESTIONS THAT EVERY INTELLIGENT CHRISTIAN MUST ANSWER), which indicate the name of a video that can (at present), be downloaded from YOUTUBE and viewed by means of either YOUTUBE or REAL PLAYER. If at the end of said phrase, there is a number enclosed by another parenthesis, i.e. (3), it indicates de number of related videos. These videos are pertinent to the subject-matter being presented, and are suggested to be viewed as they are mentioned within the text. These videos are examples, and/ or explanations that may further clarify the referred issue. If you rather see them at some other time, the book content is nonetheless complete, but you surely might miss useful, intelligent and complementing material.

INTRODUCTION

The title of the book *Indelible Mark*, refers to what (some) Jesuits say; "Give me a boy until he becomes seven years old, and I will give you back a man". The obliged question is: what kind of a man? Since I was educated by Jesuits, I can say it, by my own experience. A man that has a *religious indelible mark*, which is extremely difficult to get rid of. I was able to liberate myself, because the *religion virus* was not able to take complete hold of my mind. Since I was a teenager, I had doubts about all those "mysteries" that you are supposed to believe, without question, and I had no other choice during primary, secondary and prep schools.

But what am I saying? An *indelible mark* can be erased using sandpaper, for example. It is more rather utilizing liquid nitrogen (-196 centigrade) to penetrate deep in the brain, and becomes extremely difficult to get rid of.

A baby is baptized. When he becomes seven, he makes his first communion. A few years after, he gets confirmed. All of these acts take place when the child does not have yet his mind mature. That constitutes mental abuse, and I will tell you why. All of these actions took place simply because the place and the parents happen to follow a certain religion, by pure chance. Of the hundreds of existent religions, which is the only one true? The one that each child was indoctrinated into. What a magical and coincidental happening. This book explores profoundly the damage that religions cause to the faithful and believers.

ONE

Religious Indoctrination at school and its mirror at home

I was reared within a very catholic family. Consequently, I received education from a Jesuit school, which was considered to be one of the best, while it maintained its doors open. It was closed some years later when some internal problems developed (liberation theology). Today sits there an exclusive mall site, with apparently successful stores. Thus, in our: "Mexico lindo y querido" (Beloved and pretty Mexico, as a very popular song goes), *a very good school is torn down*, to be replaced by…, yes indeed, an elegant mall, ¿what else could a greedy mind could envision?

While the Asiatic people (specially Chinese), build huge universities, in Mexico we close quality schools, bring the edifice down and then make sure that, at least in that site, no new secular school could be build. Also, Chinese, know how to take advantage of their universities, since the alumni stay at the campus for an average of twelve hours, either taking lectures, or at the library, this is why, they have surpassed us, and will very soon, take over easily our "culture" (not to mention our economy), while the teachers' corrupt leader, utilizes her vast magisterial power to distribute, among the children at public schools, propaganda regarding her political party. The only thing that matters her, is to obtain more power. Always much more. Without limit.

Let the "great" "Television Autonomous University" at the sewage TV channel (Telebisa's Star channel) take over the education of the entire population, where courses are imparted, leading in very short time, to masters and even doctorates degrees regarding; daily political campaigns that look like interviews, acted kidnapping rescues, soap operas regarding "important matters" such as; how to be untrue, how to commit treason, how to become very aggressive, − to your own family −, (especially towards wives), how to become a drug dealer, as well as, several other "penitentiary" affairs, that a huge audience, previously very well conditioned, can't wait to watch and reclaim the daily presentations.

The Chinese are "only" good at matters that are important to progress, such as science, that turns out to be quite "boring" to our population, as well as, the manufacturing of literally everything that is manufacturable. The U.S. foolishly created a manufacturing potency, becoming themselves a service economy, thus losing its predominance. Thus, in accordance with our idiosyncrasy, let's continue our path towards the precipice.

My own evaluation of said school was outstanding, except for the compulsory catholic "indoctrination", that is catechism, daily rosary praying, and monthly mass attending, including confession and communion, of course. To my knowledge, there never was a single case of a pederast priest. The religion course was imparted by a Jesuit; I'll call him father Carlos, and due to the fact that I was somewhat a mischievous child, I recall two pranks: the first of them; our secular history teacher Usbaldo Vega, which presented very vivid descriptions, was talking about Napoleon at Waterloo, when he pointed his index finger very close to where I was sitting, in the first row of our classroom, I could not help grabbing his finger, which of course, provoked a generalized explosive laugh of all my classmates, and an immediate reprimand by our prefect. The second one; one Jesuit teacher, when momentarily out of the classroom, would appoint one of the best behaved pupils to take note of the not so well behaved pupils. His last name was "Espinosa" and just before he was to leave temporarily the classroom, I started singing (in Spanish, of course) "Mr. ESPANTOSA, would you appoint me to take note of the mischievous?" "Espantosa"; in Spanish means "horrible", which he definitively was. Another visit to the prefect with the corresponding reprimand. These pranks came to be known by father Carlos, who "christened" me as: "Velasco el malo" (Velasco, the bad one), since there was another "Velasco" in the same classroom, who similarly was "christened" by him as "Velasco el bueno" (Velasco, the good one). Now imagine what father Carlos would of christened me, had he seen the following drawing, which I dedicated to my mother, when I must have had barely six years of age. I cannot recall what drove me to make such a gory drawing (probably a movie). I still keep such knife that somehow ended up in our family.

I mention this because, according to his appreciation, his designation resulted prophetic, because if he christened me simply due to some childish pranks, how would he christen me, now that I have written this book that, before his eyes, and of the eyes of the church, that he represented, I should be excommunicated.

Since I was a teenager, I found very difficult to swallow the chain of "mysteries" that we were supposed to believe. Thus, I tried to maintain the minimum of participation that I could get by with. Also, as many catholic believers do, I am sure, whenever a doubt enter into their minds, it is given a quick excuse of justification, and it is rushed out of the brain, in order to avoid a confrontation with reality (10 QUESTIONS THAT EVERY INTELLIGENT CHRISTIAN MUST ANSWER). Another very strong reason for not taking an open different standing (agnostic, at least), was because I did not dare to provide a suffering, that would be intolerable to my mother, should I present her my "new" anti-religious standing.

The exaggerated religious standing of my family came from my grandmother, on my mother's side. Of course such strict behavior existed only in the feminine part of the family. My uncles were all but devout catholic, they were almost certainly agnostics, if not atheists, but in order, not to offend my grandmother, they remained quiet. I miss them all very much, they were cultured and refined and I was always learning from them. I remember very well, when they referred to Homo sapiens as: "a very nasty and filthy creature". At that time, I thought that remark to be somewhat excessive, now I have written several books, precisely to try to make a dissection of that appreciation, which now I find too lean, by considering in what condition we have degraded our planet, and our societies.

My uncle Fernando, was a civil engineer who lived mostly in Acapulco. He was in charge of the original potable water works to serve said community. He was the only uncle who graduated from college, he was fluent in English, as I was able to confirm in one book that he wrote, narrating diverse episodes that occurred during his stay in Acapulco. He was very savvy regarding the works of the English writer Somerset Maugham, which he recited frequently.

My uncle Carlos was a well-known painter, several of his large portraits are exhibited in the "Palacio National" at Mexico City (six ex-presidents and two Aztec emperors). He was often required to portrait presidents and their first ladies, as well as, notorious personalities. We, his nephews are glad to be the owners of some of his paintings regarding, portraits, landscapes and horses, his main concerns. It was he, who was more disgusted relative to the destruction of nature and unlimited growth of cities.

SELF PORTRAIT

CARLOS
TEJEDA

When painting nature (i.e. forests and/or animals) the; "Before they are all gone" mention, at the bottom and at the center would always appear in all his paintings. But he could not be any more accurate in his predictions. I just learned that his beloved "ranch" in Villa Juarez, Puebla (Las Cañadas), has recently been expropriated by the government to build ..., what else? A highway, of course. That fabulous forest property, full of tropical vegetation, hundreds of trees, beautiful flowers and even deer and countless plant and animal species will be replaced by a carpet of pavement. For how long would this road be in any use, when peak oil has arrived? Almost certainly, for not more than a very few decades.

Hasta que se los acaben ("Before they are all gone")

His late son, christened also Carlos, "inherited" his painting ability and became a fine architect. Long ago, I commissioned him a large painting (5X8 ft.) portraying the great Scottish driver Jackie Steward driving a Tyrell-Ford.

My uncle Francisco went to work to the U.S., at the Ford Motor Co., in Detroit, for several years. He told me that when Henry Ford, gave an order to remove something at his plant, and was not immediately obeyed, Ford himself would bring a big hammer and began the removal himself. I was very fond of my uncle, because he was the only uncle, that recalling that my father had died, when I was barely three months old, he was frequently looking after me. In order to awake my taste regarding good music, he gave a violin as a present, which I studied for a while, since it was not an instrument that I had selected. Years later, he gave another instrument that I liked, a trumpet (that I still keep with appreciation), which I studied for many years, until I realized that a virtuoso I would never become, probably due to an embouchure problem, and lack of talent. I hope that, at least one my grand children, can learn to play it "by heart", and become a virtuoso. That is, of course, if he happens to like it.

Fortunately, there has been, within my family, only two cases of a member working for the government, my uncle Francisco (just mentioned) who by chance of being wall to wall neighbor of Arturo Diaz Lombardo, made friends with him, so when Diaz Lombardo was appointed as Director of the IMSS (Instituto Mexicano del Seguro Social), he called my uncle to take charge of its car fleet. In one occasion, Diaz Lombardo called my uncle, and ordered him, that he would authorize the payment of salaries of a large number of inexistent employees, from which my uncle would receive his "bribe", which evidently resulted inacceptable to my uncle, and that *ended a friendship and his position in said institution.*

The other case was that of Adalberto Tejeda, who, in spite of being assigned, among other important positions, Governor of Veracruz, his only property was located at Coyoacan in Mexico City, and resulted in the only patrimony, which was inherited to his family. This kind of stories are unheard of and inexistent within the political class, where the rule, almost without exception, is unpunished millionaires crooks, who are widely respected!

I remember very well my grandmother, keeping with great pride, a small notebook in which she kept very careful account of her assistance to daily masses. Her average was at least three consecutive masses every day. When less of that number was annotated, she mentioned it with great sadness and surely guilt. According to catholic cult, the believer is supposed to attend church every Sunday. To concur daily, is certainly an exaggeration, but three masses daily, that's sick. That is to be fanatic, not a harmful one, but fanatic, nonetheless. In one occasion, when dawn came rather late, my grandmother went to her church, where she found the doors closed, so she decided to wait for the doors to be opened. A person that happened to pass by, came to her asking what she was doing there at 5:00 A.M., in front of the church. She explained that she believed to have risen at the same time as always did, and had not realized what early it was. So he accompanied to her house.

In her home, the rosary was, as could be expected, rigorously prayed daily, including the complete litany. That same custom, was exported to my mother's home. I myself, in order to be condescend with my mother, when I happened to be at home, at that particular praying time, I would accompany her. Invariably, when my mother went to church, which was a daily chore, would always take communion. What was impressive, was to watch her pray. Her factions revealed a *very intense suffering*, as if she was actually present at the crucifixion of Jesus, and that she solely was to be blamed for that crime. She absorbed, like a sponge, the guilt, that most priests preach that we all carry since the original sin. Now, if someone was good, it was she. She, widow after only fourteen years of marriage, with six children to take care of (have as many children as God sends you) worked extremely hard to rear her children, completely dedicated to work, and I know of many people that she helped. Fortunately, my father founded a business that my mother was able to run successfully, in spite of the very scarce education provided to women at the beginning of the 20 century, until we (her children), "forced" her reluctant retirement when she became 85 years old.

Thus I never understood the reason of that profound suffering, until I realized that the guilt that the church manages to induce in some people is staggering. This is another of the reasons for which I am writing this book. Maybe, just maybe, one or two, "believers" are able to read it, react, think, and get rid of the malevolence of all religions and churches. All religions, evidently, have been and continue to be man-made, and the source of great evil, and a barrier to freedom of thinking and the embracement of science, as a form of life, at least with respect to the adoption of skepticism, which will pay dividends in all areas of life. Since my mother passed away, that (self-imposed) restriction was no longer existent. But pretending is hideous, therefore I have taken the decision not to become an agnostic, but the more profound standing of an atheist. At the beginning, it can seem terrible, to say that you are an atheist, but; do you believe in the "Sun God", in "Tlaloc", "Huichilopoztli", the "gods of the Olympus", etc.? Aren't you an atheist before all those gods? And as Richard Dawkins argues; "we are all atheists, it just happens that I believe in one God less than yourself". Think about it. That drastic change based upon simple reasoning, evaluating scientific evidence, and the lecture of such books as; *The Blind Watchmaker* and *The God Delusion* both from Richard Dawkins and; *God is not Great,* from Christopher Hitchens; *Shadows of forgotten ancestors*, from Carl Sagan and Ann Druyan, as well as many others. "Proofs" of the falsity of God's existence abound, i.e., how to explain that all the religions in the world have failed miserably, after millennia of sacrifices and praying have not succeeded in diminishing, let alone eradicating wars (or any other of present human produced disgraces). In one occasion a Marist brother commented to me that; the "grace" of a single mass was infinite, but rather "zillion" masses have not accomplished a bit.

Given that "creationism" evidently has lost too much ground, apparently even within the "creationists", since they have now invented another rather silly non-theory called: "intelligent design". I ask therefore, "creationism" was not an *intelligent* creation already? If William Paley's example of a watch being necessarily designed, is it not that an "intelligent design" already? What else could it be? Don't these religious people see any inconsistency in this new posture? Evidently they don't. Paley takes as one of the best examples of design, the human eye, but Richard Dawkins explains quite clearly in his book; *The Blind Watchmaker*, how different eyes, in different stages of development, exist even today within the animal kingdom.

The existing scientific evidence, to eliminate the need for a God, in every branch of science is overwhelming, but if "believers" don't want to utilize their brains, little hope to change their minds exist. The "holy" books are stacked with myriad of false data, very simple to verify (INTELLIGENT DESIGN? WATCH IT GET SCHOOLED).

Thus, for a supporter of evolution, like myself, writing a book describing quite a bit, but not all, of the faults, errors, incompleteness, and lack of elegance, encountered in the "design" of the human body, it becomes necessary to debunk this new nonsense. Now, some readers might be thinking, why does this author dares to write about the arguably *few* "design mistakes", instead of writing about all the "marvels" of the human body? Yet, recall the God attributes (my comments are written using cursive font):

Attributes of God

Wisdom: "Wisdom is the ability to devise perfect ends and to achieve these ends by the most perfect means." In other words, God makes no mistakes (*In this first sentence, it becomes clear the previous paragraph! God does not make mistakes*).

Infinitude: Since God is infinite, everything else about Him must also be infinite.

Sovereignty: This is "the attribute by which He rules His entire creation." It is the application of His other attributes of being all-knowing and all-powerful. It makes Him absolutely free to do what He knows to be best. God is in control of everything that happens. Man still has a free will, and is responsible for his choices in life. *Therefore, if God is not responsible for all evil that happens on earth, he is still at least, totally indifferent.*

Holiness: This is the attribute that sets God apart from all created beings. It refers to His majesty and His perfect moral purity. There is absolutely no sin or evil thought in God at all. His holiness is the definition of that which is pure and righteous in all the universe. Wherever God has appeared, such as to Moses at the burning bush, that place becomes holy just for God having been there. *Well, God has showed himself very few times in the past, let alone in current times, where this has happened cero times.*

Trinity: Although, God reveals Himself in three persons, God is one and cannot be divided. All are involved completely. *For heaven's sake, how complicated, what is the need for such "mystery"*

Omniscience: "God knows everything, and His knowledge is infinite. It is impossible to hide anything from God. *If he knows all the terrible things that will happen, why does he permits the happening?*

Faithfulness: Everything that God has promised will come to pass. His faithfulness guarantees this fact. He does not lie. *Jesus said that he would show himself when invoked, but this has never happened.*

Therefore, such a being, if he existed, should be absolutely incapable, by definition, of producing the absolute least of faults, errors, incompleteness, and lack of elegance encountered in the "design" of the human body and elsewhere in nature and in the universe. But because we know that evolution has no plan, no blueprint, no goal "in mind", its resulting creatures will necessarily present faults, errors, incompleteness and lack of elegance. Nevertheless, the creationists not content with that demonstrated fallacious thinking, recently have launched the identical, but otherwise pompous title of ; "intelligent design" which asks (or rather yells), for yet another response, for this nonsense claims.

Believers of whatever religious beliefs they may entertain are free to do so, unless they try to force any part of the community, to be "educated" with those precepts, while blocking the teaching of evolution. This is actually what it is happening in many parts of the world today, and it is also the main reason why we, the believers that "religions poisons everything", as lucidly explained in Christopher Hitchens book; *God is not Great*, have to try to prevent such vicious and harmful happening (WHY ARE AMERICAN ATHEISTS SO ANGRY). Take into account that children (like myself) were and are forced to learn totally false "beliefs", that later on, are extremely difficult to get rid of.

This book presents a view of how a really caring (human) father would treat his children, compared with the treatment that we are told that we can expect from our merciful "heavenly father" (GOD CARES FOR US A LOT). Also, it will discuss a large quantity of errors of "design", that an almighty God could not possibly have performed, given that, we are supposedly created at his image. No doubt, we humans have marvelous "design" and can achieve great feats, but it is also true, that this "design" abounds with serious deficiencies, which will be discussed here.

Having around 99% of the exact same genes as our close cousins the chimps, the conclusion that can be extracted here is, that as marvelous as Homo sapiens can be, he is, *at most*, a "Deluxe chimp". Should this fact encourage, permit, or even justify, the behavior that most Homo sapiens (?) exemplify during their lifetimes, allowing greed, hate and stupidity to rule their lives? Or, we have continually failed miserably to utilize our intellect, the only feature that really separates ourselves from the rest of the animal kingdom (at least in degree). Seems to me, that we humans ought to be very thankful to the enormous luck of having being born, especially with the capacity to utilize creatively our brain. In fact, what a better way to show gratefulness that precisely performing at the best of our intelligence? Now, thankful to whom or what? Without doubt, thankful to the random events that run the universe, in other words, thankful to evolution and plain luck (THE APE THAT GOT LUCKY).

TWO

Faults, errors, and lack of elegance in the body "design" of Deluxe chimps

"One must do things the simplest
possible way, but not simpler"

Albert Einstein

William Paley, the Anglican pastor who lived in the 18th century is famous for his "watchmaker analogy" which stated briefly that; "if a watch is found, its complexity is such that it must have a designer". An animal, being a much more complex being, therefore must have also a "designer", i.e. God. That way of thinking is the basis of creationism and more recently a new wave of argument, which is basically the same trend with a new name. Unfortunately for the creationists, the "design" issue has been, and every day more evidence builds up, regarding the falsity of creationism, and "intelligent design", in favor to evolution. An interesting issue: our nearest cousins, the apes, have 48 chromosomes, Homo sapiens only 46 chromosomes, if there is no proof of where the missing pair went, evolution is in trouble. Fortunately, chromosome 2 got fused, giving a very elegant explanation confirming evolution (GENOME SEQUENCING LEAVE CREATIONISTS UNABLE TO RESPOND).

In his book: "The Blind Watchmaker", Richard Dawkins maintains that should a watchmaker had existed, then it must of have been blind, because no purpose or goal is evident, with respect to the "design" of all living creatures, except to provide the survival and reproduction of the fittest individuals, taking advantage of all the small *cumulative* random mutations, which are caused by evolution, not by a "designer" blind or otherwise. I might add to Dawkins's comment, that in my view, that supposed "designer" was not only blind, but also lacked; olfactory sense, compassion, elegance and several others very desirable and inevitable treats of any given almighty God.

Although, there is no doubt, that the human animal has, in many respects, a very good "design", it is also, replete with faults, errors, incompleteness and lack of elegance, in the body "design" of the Deluxe chimps, as it will be outlined in this book. Let us ask ourselves a fundamental question; should it not, the selected being of creation, "designed" as God's image, to be equipped, with the absolute best characteristics of every animal? Utilizing a human comparison, imagine one of the best designed cars, a Ferrari, let's say. Do you find faults, errors, incompleteness or lack of elegance in any of such cars? Hardly. If in anyone of these, a defective design results, the next model will come out of the factory with a modification to correct such anomaly, and usually a better and more beautiful specimen, almost always with additional features. Always trying to improve the previous design. God had eternity to "design" his own image. Of all materials (elements) from earth, which was chosen by God, to create his master creation, at his own image? Well, unbelievable, he choose dirt, yes dirt, which by definition makes us "dirty", from our very beginning. Why this choice (of dirt) does not strike the "creationists", or the newer "intelligent design" believers as absurd, silly, and therefore, an impossible material to be God's choice? Did God really expect us to be well designed (avoid original sin, among other things) with such prime building block? In fact, why would God require any material at all, could he not create anything from nothing? Thus, it happens that science, results much more "benign" with respect to our "initial matter", that being DNA, nucleic acids, proteins, etc., aside from being essentially correct, it is not "just dirt".

Speaking of the original sin; by definition: supposedly, it was and is caused every time a baby is born. The baby, a totally innocent creature, is also presumably, marked by such heavy burden, having committed no fault whatsoever. The origin of this sin, happen (we are told to believe) when Eve became pregnant. Now, becoming pregnant is (almost) the only way to have babies, by almost every multicellular animal on earth. Why on earth, would that circumstance be a sin only for the human animal? Why that absurd condemnation? How then, could an immaculate human species exist? Why would God *design* man with an overdose of testosterone and then apply such a gruesome consequence, namely a sin and damnation? But the logic in this supposedly guilty act is flawed. At the beginning, we are told, Adam and Eve were the responsible and were punished by God, no more no less, by their kicking out of paradise. Curiously, later on, the blame and sin would be transferred to the innocent babies; the recipients, not the cause of it. In order to be consistent (but assuming, without conceding); the original sin would necessarily be blamed in the parents (as in the case of Adam and Eve), not in the babies. *The parents are the ones that would need to be baptized, not the babies.* What a convoluted work of mind, of some of the writers of the bible, that yields no logic, let alone credibility.

Well, God *necessarily* had to obtain a flawless and elegant "design" of his "special" creature the very first try, but he did not, as I will remark, as follows:

Let's start with the sense of taste. This is probably the only one of our senses, that has a much better performance than any other animal, and has been one of the main reasons for our worldwide presence, that is; we like and enjoy, and therefore eat almost anything that is or was alive, either vegetable or animal, in comparison with most other species, that have a very limited diet. In fact, we even consume products in detriment of our health, such as; alcohol, tobacco, drugs, etc. The ugly part of this sense, is that a great deal of us, every day with compulsion, eat much more than actually need, and with a quality (industrial) evidently harmful to our nature. The result is an obese current global population, of at least 1,000 million people.

Most of the people, most of the time, have "bad breath", not nice for us, but very nice business for pharmaceutical companies. Is it surprising"? Hardly, considering the highly corrosive acid (hydrochloric), chosen by God as the digestive agent.

The sense of touch. With regard to this sense, it permit us to have nice sensations, as well as terrible pain. Was it not possible for God, to inform the brain of body harm, by means other than pain? Surely other type of signal, much less severe, there must exist and could have being utilized in the "design" of his favorite creature.

The sense of smell. Given that dogs are probably the animals with the best developed sense of smell, and in order to have it, they require huge noses, we Deluxe chimps, are better off with a less prominent appendix. Also, we are better off, at least in our current time, smelling less, since a great deal of present smells are foul, due to wastes and contamination. Thus, regarding this sense, at present, we probably benefit from its limited capacity, not by a preventive "designer", but rather by evolution.

The sense of hearing. In spite of not been equipped by "design" with great sound receptors (being able to hear frequencies between 20 and 20,000 cycles only) we Deluxe chimps managed to survive, in spite of very many predators. But without doubt, it could have been a very powerful survival aid, had it been much more sensible.

The sense of sight. The sense of sight has ironically being proposed by creationists, as the paramount of complex, perfect design of "irreducible complexity" (DISPROOVING INTELLIGENT DESIGN WITH A MOUSE TRAP). Ironically, because scientists can explain why it is ill designed: –upside down and inside out -. Also scientists have encountered a variety of animals that display several of the different stages of eye development by evolution; from a few light detecting cells to complete eyes, easily verifiable by any interested person (RICHARD DAWKINS MAKES AN EYE). Due to this poor "design", we have a blind spot which our brain is capable of fix it, thanks to evolution.

It is in this sense where, if God existed, could have designed a really marvelous light detector. Because such an apparatus; – the unaided eye - should be capable of seeing the tiniest organic beings, as well as, atoms, electrons, quarks and whatever smaller particles might exist. By the same token, that same; –an unaided eye-, should be able to see clear details of the solar system, other galaxies and the confines of the universe. Or, was it not the cosmos (firmament), *created for our enjoyment*, according to the "holy" books? Thus, a well-designed eye should be able to observe the smallest particles, as well as, the more distant, without external help. This because, if it had been this way, humans could be able to contemplate, with bare eyes, the maximum work of their creator. Impossible to design? I am not suggesting something really impossible to design, such as: to "move something unmovable". Let's see a human example: who, in his sane mind, would have believed and/or accepted, 50 years ago, that a phone (weighting at most around half a pound and costing around $500.00 (very devaluated), could communicate two persons located, anywhere on earth? That such phone (i.e. Black Berry) could also, provide instantly, any information desired (Internet), play a great amount of music therein stored (Itunes) and much more functions that could not be explained, because nobody could understand (i.e. Exel). If this gadget, has been designed by human engineers, in 60 years counting from the beginning of the computers era, don't tell me that God could not perform, what I commented at the beginning of this paragraph. And if he can't, simply he would be not God, or at least, not the God of the above mentioned attributes. And what was the point of making the velocity of light have a limit? Thus, a really well "designed" eye, should provide the capability of observing the tiniest, and farthest objects, *without any external aid*. This, for the simple reason that all humans could enjoy, at the maximum, the work of their creator. The universe, for his privileged creatures, for all practical purposes, was inexistent to all the God-modeled humans, beginning to uncover it, until the last three centuries, ***thanks to science***.

An interesting question to ask is; if the earth (universe) was "created" specifically for human gratification, why there exists uncountable species that are not only a nuisance but actually a real threat to humans? What "intelligent" God created, just to name a few, spiders, scorpions and specially mosquitoes? Are they really indispensable? No other "design" of earth, not including such characters is possible? Consider a mouse, rat or cockroaches; ¿are these pests also inevitable to the living chain? No other possibilities of different harmless species could exist, or could have been "designed"? One could think that coleopterans (beetles) are God's favorite animals by observing that no less than 250,000 species, are such creatures. God must be much more of a "coleopterist" than a "humanist". Continuing with our more lethal enemies, we have to go to the microscopic level; how about the mites that we are forced to share our homes with, especially our beds, where it is impossible to get rid of them, because even the cleanest home is full of them? The least that we know, is that they cause allergy, due, among other things to our breathing of their feces. Clean "design"?

What severe distraction on the "designer" procedure, could have caused him to overlook, the very predictable result that microscopic bacteria and viruses would result catastrophic to his privileged creature? In other words, how is it possible that the tiniest molecules known could cause lethal harm to the "marvel of the creation"? But, there are those creationists that propose the absurd idea of diseases being created not by God but by sin (DISEASES ARE CREATED BY SIN NOT GOD). Regarding children's illness, by definition innocent creatures, assuming that ignorant statement true, then the conclusion turns out to be that God is, to put it mildly, extremely unjust. *But if diseases are caused by sins, why do we have an immune system built-in?* Here is another contradiction which the creationists "explain" by arguing that sins permitted a mutation to develop the "noble" viruses to become harmful to humans. This argument utilizes a word "mutation" which comes from evolution theory, thus: creationists believe in evolution or not?

Similar to many other instances during the last century, the Catholic Church has been forced to "change his standing", - accept the scientific truth - after centuries of stubborn ignorance, and in innumerable occasions, deadly to the scientists. Pope John Paul II in his encyclical *Humani Generis* (1950) finally accepted evolution by declaring; that there is no contradiction between evolution and faith, but rejects a materialistic explanation of the human "soul" (THE BLIND WATCHMAKER 1/5 thru 5/5). Thus, actually only accepted a "half-truth". But, it turns out to be, that such recognition is totally opposed to the story of the creation of Adam and Eve by God. Here we have another concession to science by the church, more than a century after the postulation of the evolutionary theory, proving the bible wrong again, but which causes neither church clergymen, nor believers to bat an eyelash. No doubt the brainwash they have diehard.

The secretions of the Deluxe chimp (as well as, the rest of all animals) go from "simply" a nuisance to absolutely nasty, filthy and disgusting. The purpose of this section of the book, is to point out diverse designs of our body, that show clearly, at least, a lack of "elegance" within said architecture. The proponents of "intelligent design" should try this suggested new name (Deluxe chimp) and try to explain "intelligent and *__elegant__* design", after reading this book. It has always surprised me, that our own body, when an exposure of any inner part occurs, most people (perhaps except physicians), will show an out of control revulsion, frequently followed by fainting or vomiting of the viewer. Why do we find our own open body so disgusting? The "exposed image" of God excites loathsomeness?

Let's start top-down by examining our head. Here we find *d*andruff or the particles of dead skin that are a nuisance. Other head problems are either greasy or dry skull, deficiencies which probably contribute to the loss of hair in men. Sweat will be mentioned later. Parasites will also be treated later.

The eyes produce probably our only secretion, which is normally not disgusting, because it is mostly "salty" water and also is odorless.

Our ears grow everyday a layer of ear wax, that thickens and becomes very hard, and problematic to get rid of, except whenever (rather infrequent) the need for an otolaryngologist is required. That dry ear wax is rather repulsive. Our ears, when we grow old, also begin to grow hairs which look very ugly.

In (from) our nose, the secretions when healthy become worse, compared to the preceding secretions, but when sick from a cold they become really nauseating, let alone contagious. From the nose, also begin to grow hairs which look very ugly. Why does these hairs continue to grow in nose and ears and the hair from our head, does not keep growing in men, after certain age? Why do they grow there, and not in the head, specially for the bold? It is likely, that some readers may be considering that I am already too "picky", that really, it doesn't matter, so I would like to remind the attributes of God above listed, this one, at least: "God cannot make mistakes".

Sweat works somewhat effectively by reducing the temperature of our body, but sometimes our clothes become very wet, which becomes a nuisance. Sweaty hands are not fun when we are introduced to other people. The worst part is that sweat smells rather foul. But if you ask the manufacturers of odor-control products, they will surely say that it is one of God's best "design" features. Let's compare the best creature from divine creation and one of the best man made wonders: a Lamborghini: the cooling system of Homo sapiens has just been described above. Now, imagine that you are comfortable sitting in said automobile and suddenly, because of the need of cooling, the seats, steering wheel, etc. start to get wet. What the hell!, you would scream. What kind of "intelligent design" was used here? See my point?

The saliva from our own mouth is repulsive even to oneself, that is, not considering people in love, so if you take food out of your mouth, once it has been salivated, you will not, very likely, place it again in your own mouth.

Even though not related to secretions, it is worth to mention here a couple of additional errors: one being the size of our jaws which are too small to fit all of our molars, which causes several visits to the dentist office by large number of people. The other error being, since no automatic cleaning was provided, the difficulty in carrying out a thorough and easy cleaning of our denture due to the teeth being too close or too far apart. Very good "design" from the dentists' perspective.

Phlegm are even more disgusting, and we normally have to get rid of them fast, or sometimes we are forced to swallow them. With so many uneducated people in the world, all of us, that don't spit, find the sight of phlegm of the streets uttermost nauseating.

Some forty years ago it was produced a very interesting film; "The Andromeda Strain", which deals with a story regarding a very lethal virus, supposedly coming from the Andromeda galaxy (actually, it had been "produced" by the military, who else? The scientists summoned to study the situation, the actual cause and the cure and prevention of a global epidemic, are sent to an ultra secret military laboratory, specially designed for such or similar contingencies. The first step that all the scientists involved are to take is: to "clean one of the most dirty creatures in our world", –that is: humans-, and if I remember well, they were required to take, at least four cleaning steps after a thorough bath. One of the steps consisted of being submerged completely, in a very strong antiseptic solution and during the last step their skin was completely removed by a sort of "toasting" procedure. Although this procedure is presented in a movie, it appears to be an appropriate procedure to make our body (skin, at least) "really clean". All that trouble to remove only the exterior parasites that we carry every day of our lives. Inside of our body, surely many millions of bacteria and viruses roam freely, most of the time anyway, until some of them "wake up". Yes, I know that some bacteria are indispensable, such as the resident in our digestive tract, but even considering its benefits, is it a clean "design"? No alternative of a better "design" occurred to God? Unless, of course, all microbes are created by our sins.

The two organs that produce the most nauseating of our "secretions", which actually are really wastes, are considered next:

The first organ, is in charge of reproduction. It seems to me, that if we reproduce by utilizing the very same organ and duct, that we must use to get rid of our liquid wastes, it is a very degrading "design". In other words, if our liquid waste comes out via the same "ducts" as our babies (sperm and birth), does that not imply, that babies are also some kind of "waste" products? Was it too difficult, to at least, provide a "cleaner" different specialized "designed" duct? With regard to sex, with all the benefits due to the variety of individuals that may result, since the Deluxe chimp has been equipped with not enough large prefrontal lobes and too much testosterone, the result is a world with a great deal of violence, child abuse, incest, rape, etc. which a real magnificent "designer", could of easily have prevented somehow.

God's greatest goofs (or could these possibly be "intelligent design" features?): sex and greed: It can be easily proved that earth without sex and greed could be an immensely agreeable place to live. Just examine the daily news. What do you find? Well, all sorts of sex related crimes: passion murders, prostitution, incest, rapes, child abuse, child pornography, pederasts, etc., or at least major injustices, that cause broken families (with innocent children suffering the consequences), related to these two great vices, singly or in combination. Let us not forget, that our sex glands and their piping, on both sexes, are so prone of cancer.

What a different situation, if we consider sex and greed as evolutionary processes, with no moral considerations.

With respect to greed, just to mention an example: in our garden we have two nearby drinking bottles for hummingbirds. Each bottle has four drinking orifices. It is extremely rare to see that two hummingbirds are simultaneously drinking from the same bottle. One of them (surely the stronger) would chase away furiously the other one. This would indicate that the "greed gene" is present, and very aggressively active in this bird species. My reflection is that if at bird level, greed is "stamped" with such vicious results, what can we expect from the Deluxe chimp? Well, exactly what we see in our world today, a few multibillionaires and a few hundred multimillionaires that control world economics. Here follows a very interesting comparison (before the U.S. crisis) of some of these two multibillionaires (I received this article by email, but I do not recall the author/sender, but it is available in Internet):

Prodigal sons: Gates and Slim, Slim and Gates

"With 59 billion dollars in his pocket, Carlos Slim is today the richest man on earth, and until life in other planets is discovered, he is the richest man in the universe. The other side of the coin, is that, there are also 59 million poor Mexicans, that is; for every thousand dollars in Slim's checkbook, there is an impoverished fellow citizen that cannot cover his basic needs. This situation was foreseeable, it was only a matter of time, sooner or later, Slim would surpass Bill Gates, Warren Buffet, the Arab Sheikhs, and the richest European families. At this pace, he will outreach them altogether. Mexicans are prone to superficial analysis, but the only resemblance between the two is the amount of their fortune. Slim has 59 billion, Gates has 58 billion.

Aside from that, Bill Gates changed the world, Carlos Slim did not. Bill Gates and his company Microsoft has registered more than a thousand patents, the companies of slim none. Thanks to Bill Gates hundreds of industries have flourished and millions of business all over the world. On the contrary Slim has caused the closure of businesses like no other. Bill Gates has made history and is well known and respected worldwide, Slim is far from his fellow citizens celebrating his success, we suffer him in our own wallet.

Bill Gates succeeded against all odds, in the country more competitive in the world, fighting powerful consortiums and politicians who saw Microsoft as the enemy to defeat. Slim make his fortune under the cover of the Mexican government, obtaining juicy contracts from the public administration and with monopoly concessions within the Mexican market. Bill Gates is the son of competitive competition and father of globalization. Carlos Slim is the son of tight monopolies that provide extraordinary profits, which he utilizes to acquire other markets.

Bill Gates stands for the American dream, a college dropout, that started his business at his parent's garage and thanks to his uncanny ability, good strategy and one or two strokes of good luck, he launched himself to unsuspected heights. Carlos Slim, on the contrary, stands for the Mexican dream, to have politicians as friends, contacts at the highest levels, latchkey right to where the juicy business are granted under a veil of suspiciousness.

Since Bill Gates started his upward carrier, the U.S. followed suit; it can be said, with almost certainty, that what is good for Bill Gates, is good for the U.S. With Slim, is exactly the opposite, since Slim started to accumulate his fortune, Mexico has been in trouble, in the form of; depression, devaluation, wealth concentration, holdback, and de-capitalization. The destiny of Bill gates and the U.S. are in direct proportion, in the case of Slim the destiny is in inverse proportion. When Slim does well, Mexicans do very poorly, as opposed to the situation with Gates.

Microsoft is the most respected American company, it is the icon of the enterprise development, and the most widely desired company to work for. Telmex, on the contrary, breaks all records of complaints in the Consumer bureau, which also works for Slim.

Carlos Slim's fortune constitutes 7% of the Mexican PIB. Gates would have to own a fortune of 500 billion, ten times as much as he has now, in order to concentrate as much wealth as Slim owns now.

Finally, Gates just announced that he will leave a just amount for her daughter, so she can live with comfort in the future. The rest of his fortune will be donated to beneficiary institutions. Slim is going to leave his fortune to his children, grandchildren, grand grandchildren, and as many following generations as he can.

Neither Gates nor Slim are to be blamed for the outcome of their fortunes and lives. Both played under their systems well, Gates with the system of free market and transparency, Slim with the system of corruption and concentration of power and wealth.

Thus, the logic conclusion of this analysis is that if Gates had been born in Mexico, he would never have achieved what he attained in the U.S. Somebody would have tripped him, blocked him, either government offices or some overbearing businessman, theft, smuggling, piracy, etc. If Gates had been born in Mexico, he would have neither created Microsoft, nor changed the world. The opposite is also true, If Slim had been born in the U.S., he would have been, at most another business owner, and maybe not even that, maybe a bank clerk, retired and driving a mobile home all across the U.S.

But the "should have been", does not exist, so the only real resemblance between Bill Gates and Carlos Slim is that both are the prodigal sons of the political and economic systems that rocket them upwards".

The above comparison shows a really bizarre behavior, I refer, of course, at Gates' behavior, if he really does what he said he will. Slim's behavior, is, of course the typically greedy guy taken to the furthest possible extreme, but it resembles otherwise the normal Deluxe chimp behavior. Bill Gates understands that he will not take even a penny when he leaves this earth, and providing a "just" wealth for his daughter is enough, the rest of his overwhelming fortune to be donated to help somehow to make the world a better place. Slim seems to believe that he either will live forever, or that he will be able to take his fortune along, or, that his also absolutely greedy descendants still don't have sufficient wealth.

Returning to the last organ to consider, is really the most disgusting of any animal, much worse for the Deluxe chimp, because we are more conscious about it. The following two paragraphs consider, no doubt, the ugliest of all animal activities, and therefore the reader might opt for skipping it if he (she) might feel offended or believes it to be of bad taste. My intention is only to point out, to my consideration, the worst part of the "design" of all animals, and in particular of the Deluxe chimp.

Imagine somebody enjoying his meal (digested by the very powerful hydrochloric acid) when suddenly sometime afterwards, he (she) feels an irrepressible desire and vomit comes rushing out with a tremendous force. No doubt that, if the food is somehow unsuitable for assimilation, it has to be discarded, but there are different ways of doing it. The actual "design" results utterly disgusting, is this really the best way to solve this problem? It can induce other people nearby to vomit themselves.

Sorry, time has come to talk about animal excrements. Could God possible design shit? Or was it the result of sins also? To me (and probably to most people) the most unpleasant moment of the day is when I have to defecate, when almost invariable I ask to myself: "Who in hell designed this"? Why on earth God would choose to be a mammal? Now, remember that from our very first meal, the day we are born, until the day we die, we carry within us constantly that extremely unpleasant fecal matter. And how about small children (or old aged incontinent adults) having to wear diapers that confine their manure (outside of their body) and are forced to carry it with them until they learn how to use underware, sometime after two years of age. Which amounts to the only solution, that the Deluxe chimp has been able to implement, in order to correct said "design mistake".

Actually, as some of us know, nobody "designed" that, that was evolution's solution to get rid of the waste product. And that is why, it did not have to be elegant at all, only efficient, and efficient, it is. Except when you get peritonitis, that very frequently brings along your death. What I do, and strongly recommend to the readers to consider it to acquire the following habit (if you do not have already): only when unavoidable utilize public or other people's bathrooms. This can be very easily done, if you have accustomed yourself to defecate everyday immediately before taking your shower. Another interesting recommendation, the use of tissue paper evidently cleans very poorly, so why not go directly to clean yourself under the shower, and also save some money by only buying some tissue paper for "emergencies" or visitors. A reminder to the people that think too much of themselves, such as millionaires, politicians, high-level clergy, and stars (of any type of entertainment), don't forget that all of us (yes, you included) are Deluxe chimps, that carry an intestine always dirty with fecal matter.

God most have known that practically every women on earth (as well as most men) would be unsatisfied with her normal appearance, so why not "design" women with makeup (or equivalent) built in? The immense amount of time and money spent every single day and night could be saved.

Another "could have been" idea: how about utilizing the practically unlimited energy of the sun, in recollecting units (or our skin), around our body (such as solar cells) as the means of providing "power" for the Deluxe chimp. Even more sophistication could be obtained by additionally employing a sort of photosynthesis, which would completely eliminate the need for hunting (killing), cooking, eating, defecating, etc. Was this too advanced technology for God?

With regard to our limbs (as well as other parts of our bodies), why is it that no automatic replacement takes part? Why does salamanders experience this? Is it because salamanders are somehow more important than the Deluxe chimp? Why God did choose that otherwise "irrelevant" animal for such really amazing feat? Or given that it is very difficult to understand so valuable feature of said animal, why God, at least, has not ever grown an amputee member regardless of the amount of praying? (10 QUESTIONS THAT EVERY INTELLIGENT CHRISTIAN MUST ANSWER) (I BUILT A PRAYER AMPLIFIER). *Only one* of such (proved) miracles, viewed worldwide could immediately convert every atheist, agnostic, schismatic, apostate or otherwise non believer, as well as believers of other faiths. It is a wonder why it has not yet occurred to God. Too late now. In fact, very likely, rather soon, the Deluxe chimp could be able to perform said "miracle" on humans. How could this extraordinary feat be accomplished? "Simply" by manipulating the corresponding Hox gene. In the book; *OXYGEN The Molecule that made the World* from Nick Lane, PhD in biochemistry, he writes: "Having extra, dispensable, body parts makes specialization and complexity easier to achieve. For example in the ancestors of the arthropods, the large group to which modern insects and crustaceans belong, a small change in the workings of a Hox gene could cause new legs to sprout on previously bare segments, and then these evolved into antenna, jaws, feeding appendages and even sexual organs". These and many more experiments have already been performed mostly with "Drosophila Melanogaster" mosquitoes.

A very interesting question to ponder is; why would God choose poisons to create/maintain life?, such as oxygen. The chemical table contains near a hundred elements and God could have created an infinite additional number if needed. If Linus Pauling, eminent biologist, and, besides other amazing feats, the recipient of two Nobel prices, would propose to us that, water is formed by oxygen and nothing else, it would provoke serious doubts about his chemistry knowledge. Thus, if God, the scientist of scientists, tells us; that man is made out of dirt, being that water is the main constituent of flesh, by far, that produces serious doubts about the knowledge that God has regarding human constituents, which, evidently, is not reasonable. But what it becomes reasonable, once again, is that, man, not God, was the provider of the text for the bible. Period.

During the presumptuous bread multiplication miracle, Jesus supposedly provided enough bread (out of only five pieces) for about five thousand followers. The sentence: *Give us this day our daily **bread***: is literally a part of the prayer that Jesus himself teach us. As I mentioned previously, it is not hard to take notice how God utilizes several poisons and/or hazardous substances (oxygen, hydrochloric acid, etc.) which is very difficult to understand.

¿How is it possible, that God, not only utilized improper substances for the "design" of the human body, but also, as one of the main food products, recommended and provided by him?

I used to take sleep pills daily, during many years, in order for me, to be able to sleep at nights. Some nights, after having cereal (Cheerios), or a piece of bread, and going to bed, I started to feel very anxious, at such degree, that I had to rise from the bed, and go to read for a long while, before returning to bed. Recently, I bought a book: *Grain Bread* by David Perlmutter, which permitted me to realize what the problem was: ¡Wheat!, that was it. To be able to test anything: what a wonder. The following night, aware of the poison that I was taking, I had a salad for a night cap, I took no pill, and went to sleep. ¡A perfect night! as well as, all the following. I have never taken any pill again, provided that I consume no wheat products, which I evade, with only a few exceptions, during the early part of the day. Now, if you are able to think, deduce, and provide conclusions, you, inevitable, have to come to the fact that, it is absurd that God would provide such nonsense as stated above. Given the importance of bread, within the Catholic religion, exemplified by the proclaimed bread multiplication miracle, and nonetheless, the Holy Father prayer, one could assume that the foodstuff, par excellence, could neither be contaminated nor purposely modified to become a poison, due to the gluten, that the NonSanto racket, by means of modifying the structure of the wheat genome, which one could also assume, that it would not be permitted by God, to be altered by humans (again complete free will, at expense of billions?) But, as mentioned in some other part of this book, whatever, or whoever does not exist, cannot do, undo, or prevent anything!

Another interesting question is: why God created ageing? If animal's bodies are capable of repairing themselves, why this marvelous process stars to deteriorate in only a few decades until finally ceasing altogether? Because we could, if as such "designed", cease to exist, but still in full use of our body and mind.

Why not eternal life from the beginning? To create humans to live for a few decades on earth, as a result of the original sin, which God must of have known that would happen, due to the poor "design" of our brain and the excess of testosterone, and to his omnipotent knowledge, is, at least, pitiful for two reasons: the first reason is that since the universe is expected to last for more than 100 billion years, to "design" humans at his own image, to last, at most, around a century seems rather an extreme waste. Why an omnipotent father did not create us directly as spirits already residing forever in heaven, thus eliminating painful happenings, such as illness, aging and eventual and unavoidable dead? There is, according to the bible, ample variety of beings to choose from such as; angels, seraphs, cherubs, archangels. But let's remember that, even some angels were ill-designed, as when the most cherished of God's cherub, Lucifer also disobeyed him. So, the two most important creatures, creations of God, result ill designed, still not enough proof of lack of "intelligent design" ability, or even better, "proof" of the inexistence of God? Being myself a mathematician, I know what a proof exactly means, nevertheless, I will use the word "proof" without apostrophes, which will then mean the world "proof" as we commonly use it in daily use, not in its rigorous manner utilized in said science.

A few years back, the TV program *The Invaders* was transmitted, where David Vincent tried mostly unsuccessfully, to warn humans against the invaders, from an extinguishing planet from another galaxy. These aliens, adopted the human physique, so they were almost indistinguishable from humans, except that they had a rigid little finger (here showing very little imagination) and no pulse, because they had no heart. But my reason to write in this book about it, is that these aliens had an exceptional death. When these creatures died, they would immediately vaporize. That permitted no worms devouring flesh, no messy remains, no pestilence. Now, if we have to die, why not do it as elegant as possible? How was it possible for a TV writer, to imagine such kind of "ideal" death, and not possible for God to "design" his image, with such elegant termination of life?

It is said, that there is evil on earth, because man was created with complete "free will". Man discovered since the XVII century that engines were not reliable enough, to allow themselves "free will", for the simple reason that they would destroy themselves, due to runaway speeds. Thus, something for controlling the speed of the rotating engine, was found necessary; therefore, a device known as a "governor" was invented. A "governor", or *speed limiter*, is a device to measure and regulate the speed of a machine, such as an engine. The classic example is, the centrifugal governor known as; the Watt or fly-ball governor, which uses weights mounted on spring-loaded arms, to determine how fast a shaft is spinning, and then uses proportional control, to regulate the shaft speed. Automobiles are a common application of governors, and modern automobiles may be equipped with such mechanisms, for various reasons. There are two types of automobile governors; one limiting the rotational speed of the engine, the other limiting the speed of the vehicle. In small, low power applications, governors are used to protect the engine from damage, due to excessive rotational speed.

Therefore a ***complete*** "free will" for the Homo sapiens as the excuse for evil and the destruction of the planet earth constitutes an "*un*intelligent design". If man was able to design a governor, to ensure that his engine designs would avoid destroying themselves, was it too difficult, or rather impossible task for God? Didn't God know that his cherished creature, created at his image, was ill "designed" that inevitably would fail hopelessly. What's the use of being almighty then? Because the Deluxe chimp performs runaway situations in whatever evil behavior is possible, and by definition positive feedback (run away), will always cause the eventual destruction of such systems. Examples? ; Abrupt global climate change (see video index) which everyday appears to be an inescapable catastrophe, probably at most, starting at the middle of our century. Population growing at explosive levels, currently around 7.5 billion "destructors" (some exceptions), and some conservative estimates indicate a population of 9.5 billion by the end of the century, depending, of course, in the type of measures taken, if any. If now we have become a tremendous threat for the planet and ourselves, just imagine the absurd scenario from now on. The total lack of sensibility toward our "relatives"; plants and animals, which results in countless species already gone, and countless others in danger of extinction.

Fine-tuned: in his book *GOD a failed hypothesis*, Victor J. Stenger arrives to very appropriate conclusions regarding the "fine-tuned" constants that supposedly permitted the firmament (the universe) to develop, as it did, having, of course, humans as the consent creatures of creation. If anything, the universe is (at least, most of it) absolutely incompatible with life, perhaps with the exception of microbes.

Earth, except for a very narrow margin above its surface, is also completely incompatible with life of the animals "images of

God", again with the exception of microbes. But, contrary to a well "designed" being, *precisely* where an ample margin of boundaries would have been desirable, an *extremely* fine-tuned limits abound. Let's analyze some of the following human constraints:

Body temperature. The normal range should not vary, at most, two degrees centigrade, otherwise, a life threatening condition is likely to arise.

External temperature. We humans, feel comfortable within a very narrow range of external temperature (15 to 25 degrees centigrade). Given that, it appears to exist in nature the range; from absolute cero, by international agreement, it is defined as 0K on the Kelvin scale, and as −273.15°C on the Celsius scale, to hundreds of millions (or more?) in space, what was the point, when "designing" the favorite creature to feel comfortable at such an extremely short range, that is not found frequently on earth?

Life span. The cave man, which was how the original Homo sapiens developed (some 200,000 years ago), or if the creationist feel better, six thousand years ago, humans lived an average of only thirty years. Today, in the XXI century, the life expectancy is of around 75 years (science, thank you very much), but with increasingly and generalized old age ailments, if we continue to be alive. "Intelligent design" followers, is this really a good design? Take into account, that according to the book: *The five ages of the Universe* by Fred Adams & Greg Lauglin, that the universe is likely to last at least 101 billion years. This amount compared to 30 years gives an idea of a no better design as the human engineers designed things (like refrigerators), during the middle of the XX century, to last about thirty to fifty years.

Body chemistry: Human Fine tuning of body chemistry? You bet. Today, any lab analysis that you take, shows the low and high values that are normal, outside of that very narrow band, you are in trouble. Again, why was necessary to "design" with such a fine tuning, when a much more ample range would had proven to be much more "healthy".

As mentioned above, it strongly appears to be that God, if he exists, has as his second best creature the beetle, and the first, undoubtedly, the microbes and viruses. For the microbes are the real benefactors of the universe. The universe, that absolutely enormous and very rapidly expanding entity, was created for the tiniest living organisms, for they thrive everywhere. Apparently, they are very happy in the coldest or hottest places, aerobic or anaerobic, on earth or water, inclusive within all sorts of poisons. Should it not, these last mentioned characteristics, correspond to the chosen creature, image of God?

Check engine warning; Another function highly convenient that occurred to the human engineers, but not considered by the creator, is the "check engine" warning light, now in use in most modern vehicles, at least within some prices ranges, that even when it does not identify the specific problem, at least, indicates a problematic engine, that needs to be revised. Don't you agree that this is an "absolutely indispensable" feature that was not included? Indeed not only a corresponding; "Check body", was necessary, but a rather specific; "Check lungs", "Check heart", etc. Was it an insurmountable effort to God?

Emergency switch: The Deluxe chimp body, had it been well "designed", should have been incorporated with an emergency life ending capability. Or, is it reasonable, charitable or logic that a conscious animal, given an abnormal, undesirable, cruel situation, plain extreme exhaustion, or very painful anemic or bodily suffering should be kept alive against his will? Horses with a broken leg are put to death, thus liberating further unnecessary suffering for the animal. Space vehicles which deviate from its programmed course are similarly destroyed. Long ago human engineers have designed switches that prevent a dangerous situation. Did it not occur to God that circumstances could eventually happen to his preferred creature that could make living undesirable and/or unbearable to said being? God could have made use of a feature utilized in computers today, where a confirmation of a requested very important command (say, erase a file) would prevent undesired results.

We can therefore conclude, that the body of the Deluxe chimp works fairly well for a variable brief period (a few decades), but its slow deterioration starts shortly after adolescence. The several "design" errors or omissions above mentioned are definitely not compatible with the definition of God. But if we consider that "design" as provided by evolution, we find a really wonderful outcome, given that, it is the best solution encountered (so far), always advancing from what already was there, without the possibility of starting anew. Evolution: thank you very much, not to God, but rather to nature, that has "fabricated" everything.

There are many scientific papers and books related to the many severe threats that we have imposed to ourselves. The book; *Our Final century,* by the Astronomer Royal, Sir Martin Rees, calculates that the civilization of the Deluxe chimp, has only a 50-50 chance of making it to the 22nd century. Dr. Carl Sagan was very frequently preoccupied and discussed in public, and within his many books, the danger that we pose to ourselves (ONE OF CARL SAGANS' MOST PERTINENT MESSAGES TO HUMANITY).

The only correct name for our capability of destruction is as; "the worst plague ever", quantitatively and qualitatively. Not a very nice qualifier, for God's special creation on its own image.

THREE

Religious confrontations

"Had I been present, at the time of creation, I may have given
some useful ideas, for the better organizing of the universe"

Alfonso X (the wise)

IMAGINATIVE CARICATURE: a fellow appears seated
comfortably in his armchair, enjoying his preferred *drink,*
in front of the television set, and with an amazing philosophy,
based in Descartes, but adapted to our present-day civilization, is
reasoning: "I EXIST, THEREFORE I BETTER DO NOT THINK".

On one hand, the universe (except for a very limited area
proper for life existence) is a totally hostile environment to allow
life (at least, as we know it). On the other hand, given the status of
the earth and how the Deluxe chimp has taken care of, Alfonso X's
sentence, has complete relevance. I myself, far from being a wise
man, with the risk to make mistakes, I dare to expose my point
of view in some of the useful suggestions for the best organizing
of the universe, some of which may coincide, with the views that
Alfonso X himself had imagined.

If God created the universe for our command, appreciation
and enjoyment, why is it absolutely hostile? Some creative design
could have allowed his favorites creatures to survive traveling (not
even our own satellite was possible to visit), even at the velocity
of light to be able to travel, at least, to the closer stars. That way

for an infinite space, for practical intentions, we are anchored to this little planet, at least, for the time being. After de oil era, it's very doubtful that any more space adventures will be permissible. I do not see the intelligent design. Where is the intelligent design? The photos obtained by the Hubble telescope (among others) are so absolutely amazing, that the mere absence of mention, of the greatness of the universe in the *holy* book, is proof that it was written by men. Or the more magnificent divine work, (and possible proof of his existence) may it have slipped God from mentioning it, in his holy book? Not even he mentions the solar system, in the aforementioned book. What the faithful do not realize yet, is that science has disclosed how impressively colossal the cosmos is, much more immense than the God that they believe that exists. They are pleased with a tiny God (*firmament* instead of (near) infinite cosmos).

Now, regarding the only place that enables life (that we know of), is a continuous threat to its inhabitants, with events such as: earthquakes, forest fires, tsunamis, flooding, comets, asteroids, predators, bacteria, virus, etc. What intelligent, capable *human* father, would place his children on such place? Had an almighty father been unable to decide of a safer place for his especial creatures? Regarding the natural disasters, we are so unprotected, but at least, we can sometimes become relatively alert to them. Regarding the millions of different microscopic creatures, we are in total disadvantage. Had not been thousands of scientific investigations, there would be dead persons by the thousands (millions?), with the appearing out of every epidemic, or even worse, a pandemic. Was God without knowledge that such creation would damage his beloved creatures and cause them untold suffering? Or the faithful, in reality believe that these hateful destructive creatures, small monsters, come into being by sins? (DISEASSES ARE CAUSED BY SIN NOT GOD).

Even more strange is the fact that portions of bacteria and virus DNA are found in our own DNA. Talking about DNA, there is another proof of God's existence, that the creator missed the opportunity to mention DNA in the sacred book. Was it too complicated for him to mention the scientists' names and the year of such discovery? Who then would have the slightest doubt regarding the sacred writings? Is it really, *asking too much, only to give to his creatures a verifiable prophecy, is it? Evidently, it is.*

Aside from the apparently useless portion of the chromosomes (*junk* DNA), having an additional chromosome, which is clearly dangerous, for example, to have a 21 extra chromosome, provokes the Down's syndrome. In the book; *Adam's Curse* by Bryan Sykes, who is professor of genetics at Molecular Medicine's Institute at the University of Oxford, he declares; "The human chromosomes are not, stable and reliable. They can break-up or duplicate, or do an enormous quantity of rare things, and what's more, do it with an alarming frequency. If chromosomes be our genetic diagram's deposit, they are worrying fragile".

It follows a dissertation, *in my own words*, by some Perry Marshall that I received via email, from his series "Where did the Universe Come From?" In part 4, he comments that if you can read his contention, he can prove that God exists, by means of an irrefutable proof, as follows:

You will probably not notice now the bottom line, but this email is a proof of the existence of God. Sure, looks crazy, but wait for my complete argument, until you see the evidence, just hold on, here it goes; my argument contains sentences formed by words and ultimately by letters which delivers a message that means something, and if you can read English, you can understand what the message says. Also, you can take several actions with it. You can store it in your computer as a WORD document, you can send it to a friend, and you can print it and so forth. Nevertheless, the information remains the same regardless of how you copy it or where you send it. Thus, my email contains a message, which utilizes a language, which is not dependent in the medium which was used to send it. Messages are not made by matter, even though they can be carried by matter, such as, printing this email on a sheet of paper.

Messages can be carried by energy (like the sound of my voice.), but they are not energy. Messages are not made by any material. Information can be transmitted and copied in many ways, but the meaning remains the same. Very importantly, messages can be in English, Spanish or Japanese, or in many other mediums.

Every cell in our body contains a message encoded in DNA, which is a recipe representing a complete plan for any of us.

Well, what does this have to do with a God?

Simple enough, languages, coded information and messages can only come from a mind. It's very simple, I repeat; messages, languages, and coded information only come from a mind. We can see how nature creates very interesting phenomena, but non-living things cannot create neither language nor codes.

Some people believe that life started on earth, by accident, from a "primordial soup" in the early oceans, which later on, produced enzymes and eventually RNA, DNA, and primitive cells.

But there is a problem with this theory: It does not answer the question: from where did the information come from? DNA is neither a molecule, nor is it simply a pattern. It contains chemicals and proteins, but those chemicals form an intricate language, in the exact manner that English, Japanese and HTML do. DNA has a four-letter alphabet, and structures very similar to words, sentences and paragraphs. *It has precise instructions and systems that check for errors and correct them when they appear* (I stressed this sentence).

To the individual who trumpet that life arose by itself, ask him/her: where did the information come from? I dare you to show me just one example of a language that didn't come from a mind. This is a simple question that, I have presented in public presentations and Internet discussion forums for more than four years. I've addressed more than one hundred thousand people, including hostile skeptical audiences who insist that life arose by itself without any celestial intervention. But none of them have ever been able to explain where the information came from. This puzzle is;

"So simple that any child can understand; so complex, no atheist can solve."

I disagree profoundly; Marshall´s "proof" seems flawless, similar to Paley's, but Marshall did not analyze a required further step, because Marshall is forgetting, at least one of the God`s attributes, already mentioned in this book, but that requires a reminder:

Wisdom: "Wisdom is the ability to devise perfect ends and to achieve these ends by the most perfect means." In other words, God makes no mistakes. —*The New Jerusalem Bible*

Marshall says: "DNA consists of an alphabet of four letters and structures very similar to words, phrases and sentences. ***With the proper instructions to check and correct mistakes".***

How could god "forget" to make sure that his information scheme did not contain "trash" (non-utilized, very repetitious) DNA, and mainly, that the duplication of said language could not possible contain duplication errors that would produce very important and even lethal consequences on his consented creature, created to his perfect image (and all other species) ? How can Marshall answer the fact that, DNA is a marvel, but not perfect? This riddle is; *so simple any child can understand; so complex, no believer can solve.*

Supposing that Marshall is right, I repeat the question: was it impossible for God to mention DNA in the bible, so that humanity would have at least one, but nonetheless enough PROOF that god exists. Was it too difficult for God to say; "man created from a DNA recipe", instead of "man created from dirt"?

It very well could be that a 100,000 people could not answer your question, Mr. Marshal, ¡but the 100,001 certainly could! ¿Or do you really believe in is a careless and an imperfect god?

Now then, granted that the human DNA and the chimp's DNA differ in less than 1 %. Is that small percentage of our closest relatives, so important, that could leave them without a soul and without *eternal glory?* Which seems terribly sad and unjust to me, and for a God with no trace of compassion. Our cousins received an "F" mark, with no option to improve their grade. This situation, here on earth could be debated in front of teachers, or judges, and even a lousy lawyer could crush the case, with a winning percentage close to 100 %.

Why God did supplied nipples to men? The answer appears again in the book: *Adam's Curse* by Bryan Sykes, where he describes: *how to make a man.* During the first six weeks of the fetus, visible distinction does not exist between a male and a female. As from the seventh week, it begins the formation of the differences in sexes. It is very interesting to mention that: the *sex default is the feminine* and it proceeds when the so-called Mullerian conduits (his discoverer) develop forming all of the feminine piping including ovaries and complements. If the master gene in the chromosome "Y", for some hours becomes active, the protein SRY (Sex Region in the chromosome "Y") activates several genes even in another chromosomes, activity that triggers the formation of the testicles. In a similar manner, it proceeds to produce two types of hormones: one of them proceeds to destroy the Mullerian ducts, allowing the Wolffian ducts (his discoverer) to become to be winners. The other hormone is, of course, the testosterone. If no chromosome "Y" is present during fertilization, the Mullerian ducts take precedence and destroy the Wolffian ducts: that way a female gets in line. The answer to the question of the start of the paragraph is: Evolution was the cause!

Therefore, neither man came into being from dust (Adam), nor Eve of one of his ribs, nor as I exposed above, the masculine sex, is not even prioritary. It is unfortunate to find (for the believers), one more time, that the Bible is mistaken. We, men, have nipples, due to the indicated explanation, that the female sex is the default and the priority. But proofs does not count, for whom does not want to see them, it's no use. The efficacy of *The Indelible mark* is confirmed. There exist very religious people, that in turn believe in the theory of evolution. Well; that is a contradiction: it is like believing in astronomy and astrology, or chemistry and alchemy simultaneously. Let's see; if Homo sapiens is the chimps' very close cousin, he is an ape, as in reality we are, and therefore, Adam also was so. Now then, if God created Adam to his image, it just so happens that Jesus (God) was an ape. It appears, at least to me, that the previous logical conclusion, is an aberration, and a very distasteful downgrading of God's stature, not by me, or by any scientist, but rather by the writers of the bible, which were unable to foresee, the advancement of science (especially evolution) from the XX century to our days. Why is so difficult, to find and accept the result of a simple syllogism? How does somebody can be able to deny the above consequence?

Adam had a navel, or was he an exception? How do the believing *intelligent* design/creationists or Perry Marshall answer to these questions?

All diseases are, certainly, unworthy to all animals, but there are some especially repugnant. Think about elephantiasis, leprosy, tumors, worms (tenias), etc. Why a loving God, did not have the elementary care to avoid in his creation the aforementioned repugnant diseases?

According to "the writings", *the first* disobedience to God was enough for making him angry (does God gets angry?), so much that; Adam and Eve were thrown out of paradise. First question: did not God know that the aforementioned disobedience was going to happen and therefore the punishment was too severe? The second question: since he should have known that the commented disobedience was going to happen, why he did not feel the need to improve his favorite creature, in order that, such act did not happen? The question: for the so loving and compassionate God, was it reasonable to punish *all of* Adam's and Eve's descendants extending to the ending of time? View it from the human point of view. Do you see it reasonable that if you would commit (almost) any fault, error or debt, absolutely every one of your descendants, have to pay for your oversight, ineptitude or any other reason? Evidently, it is neither reasonable, nor just. Although, that is precisely the norm that governments have copied from the bible; the public debt is to be paid by millions of completely innocent and uninformed future generations. And the punishment (among others): *"You will have to earn the bread with your front's sweat daily, the women will have to bring forth a child with pain and you will die"*. Then, it seems; that Adam and Eve were some sort of bums, not doing something useful, only resting all the time (absolutely boring, like the heaven that the church promises). Therefore, according to the "writings", God regards work as a punishment. This is a very weird declaration, especially coming from God, don't you think so? The fact is; that Homo sapiens, after becoming established in Africa, eventually learned to walk erect, modification that enforced a reduction of the birth canal in the feminine structure, which caused a painful childbirth. In like manner, his favorite creature was *designed* with a better and bigger brain, without taking this into consideration, thus: the aforementioned painful childbirth was established itself. As usual, evolution which has lasted for millions of years, *with no purpose in mind*, has the correct answers. (PEOPLE ARE NOT ANIMALS AND EVOLUTION NEVER HAPPENED).

The paragraph (previous to the three questions), translated into human behavior could be comparable to a human father that would have forbidden his children to open certain room within his house. But it happens that; the children disobey the father *once* and the following punishment emerges; the father expels his children of his home forever, curses them, withdraws all their inheritance and it applies to all of his descendants this punishment and curse: Question: Does it seems to be a benevolent and loving father this one action, or rather, the action of an absolutely crazy father and bad guy? Had it not been much simpler, to forgive this *first* disobedience, applying what Jesus teach: "Present the other cheek"? But, no, God had to send his own son to be sacrificed. Being one God, but three different persons, do they have differences as to the related with Jesus's opinion?

As a minimal sample of love of *our divine father,* for his benevolence, there was not room for providing, at least, a basic *kit,* that could consist of minimal survival instructions, when he *kicked Adam and Eve* out of Eden, such as: the form of obtaining fire, how to manufacture tools (even stone tools), how to cure injuries, how to grow vegetables, etc., Also, such kit, *would have been a proof of his existence.*

Let's talk about: the Catholic marriage. In a certain moment, the priest says something like: "What God has joined, let no man separate it". Is the force of human breaking marriages, greater than the force of God's union? The fact that this cannot be truth, is in no way evident? This is to close the mind and to accept an absurdity, without raising objections, in the least. *The indelible mark* shows itself in action again.

With respect to prayers: Is it plausible that God requires that his *little favorite animals pray* interminably? In fact, does he needs our prayers? Will he feel more self-confident or what joy can they provide him? If you are Catholic, have you asked yourself, why within a rosary; there are *only* five "Our Father's" (Lord's Prayer), and fifty prayers to the Virgin (Holly Maries)? This immediately presupposes that the virgin is more important than God. To our human level, normally it is enough to ask for one apology, at most three, to forgive almost any offense (the ones that are forgivable), thus, at the divine level, the pardon never comes. In the rosary of 55 prayers: God does not understand the very first one? *(I BUILT A PRAYER AMPLIFIER EDWARD CURRENT).*

Is it necessary to pray to a virgin? If so, to which? What is the wonder of being a virgin? I believe to be able to answer this question: that is the way of freeing Jesus from the original sin. What I do not understand, is why God would designate a form of reproduction of his preferred creature (that curiously is identical to almost all other animals), then, he turns it into the original sin, and at a later time he does not utilize it on himself? That is not logical and it is very confusing. From where did so many virgins emerge? Why are so many reports of *appearing* virgins, but not one of Jesus (for more than 2.000 years)? After all, Jesus promised to appear provided that we ask him for that. *(PROVE THAT JESUS IS IMAGINARY IN LESS THAN 5 MINUTES).*

Is it also necessary to pray to the saints, in order that they speak up for us? The C*reed* prayer says: "and for you brothers in order that you intercede for me in front of our lord", when supposedly only Mary or Jesus can talk with the *Father* directly, here is another contradiction. Evidently, no pope, cardinal, bishop, priest or pious had seen this inconsistency? My sinful brothers will achieve reducing my punishment? What, if I pray directly to the *father*, does my prayer does not reach him? Well, he is a very peculiar *father*! *(THE BEST OPTICAL ILLUSION IN THE WORLD).*

Continuing with the comparison between a human and a divine father, what loving human father ever abandons his children for life. Why has Jesus never returned? I mean, really, not as some believe in the masses. Over two thousand years have not been sufficient? Not even did he provided us with basic knowledge for the basic and vital matters to make life a little less difficult?

Finally, a *good* human father gives options to his children; the study of a certain profession, neither he obligates to marry a certain person, nor he presses them in order that they buy a house in particular (to the father's taste), etc. However, to us supposedly God's children, we are not consulted, neither the most basic, that is: if we want to be born, where we want to be born, who do we want to be our parents, what color of skin, hair, eyes, etc., we want to have. The only important option in our life that we have, and that is very relative, because it depends on many factors, as from our socioeconomic position, the country where we were born, etc., it is the one choosing of our mate. Indeed, if anyone would have been born, in a country that believes in other religion, he would be guilty, of not believing in the *three different persons and only one true God,* and would therefore be guilty of eternal punishment? *That indeed is unjust.*

You find the value of Pi = 3, in the book; *The Kings* of the *Bible*, as usual, the creationists press the point that the Bible is not a scientific book, therefore, it is not expected to find exact precision in numbers that are mentioned there. **Evidently, the Bible is not a scientific book**, *we* do not expect a dissertation, or mathematical proof of any type. What we would expect, however, it to find a correct number (I would believe that God can do that). Consider it. He lost another golden opportunity to leave behind an irrefutable proof of his existence here. Had it been enough to have established the first 500 decimals of Pi, at most, perhaps much less (4?). But for God what difference does it makes? Then, if is not a scientific book, why it dares to mention dates and/or durations of enormously incorrect epochs, than instead of trusting the book, they make many people to doubt God's existence. But, the truth is; **the Bible should be a scientific book**, given that God is supposedly; the greatest scientist, mathematician, architect, engineer, etc., par excellence. The few data that there appears, should be 100 % exact. Therefore, it proves the evidence that God did not dictate the Bible.

However, the Bible is a good book, but only for the inquisitive mind to the effect to examine absurd thoughts that millions of people believe. Because the truth is; that almost each sentence, is an invented happening, a lie, exaggeration or gross ignorance, not to mention the wrongdoings and curses there described. In this section, I am going to expand on this book, the part that narrates the creation (genesis).

The Bible, if it was truth, would have taken only *__one__* of the following words or sentences, in capital letters and underlined (which are mine), written there without a doubt, that God had been the author of the mentioned book. Being God the author, it had not been possible, not even a comma out of place, which is why my analysis will be detailed. Good: before going into details, a question (another one?) enters in my mind, the opaque motive: why Jesus chose his *writers (and apostles)* from among the more ignorant persons in the world. Why no choosing, for example, Greek thinkers, of the stature of: Plato, Aristotle, Arquimedes, Pythagoras, etc., That is, they had been the scientific originators, those who were very much apt for understanding the laws of the creation, established by the *designer?*

Now definitely, let's check the mentioned text:

Genesis 1 (Revised Version in English, but it is my translation):

God created the sky in the beginning (<u>BIG BANG</u>) and the land was a waste and empty and darkness were on that deep surface: And God's spirit moved on waters. And God said: Let's make light: And light was made. And the light was born, and God saw that it was a good thing. And so God divided the light from darkness. And God call in the light a Day, and darkness he call it Night (<u>ROTATION OF THE EARTH</u>). And there was an afternoon and there was tomorrow, one day.

And God said, let's make the firmament (which is incorrect, since the cosmos is anything, but firm), separated firmament from waters, and that they share the waters of waters. And God made the firmament (<u>13.6 BILLION YEARS AGO</u>), and it divided the waters that were down of the firmament of the waters that were above the firmament and that way it went. And God called the sky firmament (UNIVERSE or COSMOS). And there was an afternoon and a morning, the second day.

And God said: that the water under the sky come together in a place. And the dry land was put together (<u>ON TOP OF THE TECTONIC PLATES</u>): And that way it went. And God separated the dry land (<u>PANGEA</u>): and to the immediate waters he call them oceans; and God saw that it was good. And God said: let the land produce grasses, grasses seeds, and fruit trees that yield of its fruit, where they will have seeds, at the land and that way it was. And the grasses grew of the land. Grasses producing trees producing fruits, from where they are seeds (<u>GENOME</u>). And God saw that it was good. And there was an afternoon and a morning, the third day.

And God said, that the lights in the firmament from above (NUCLEAR FISSION) to divide the night be made, and that the signs exist, and seasons (TERRESTRIAL AXLE'S INCLINATION), and for the days (EARTH ROTATION); and let there be years (EARTH TRANSLATION); and that there be lights in the firmament that they give light (VELOCITY 299,792,458 km/s). And God made the big lights; the bigger light; the sun (WITH A LIFE SPAN OF APPROXIMATELY TEN THOUSAND BILLION YEARS) to govern the day, and the minor light to govern the night: Then, he made also stars (PULSARS, QUASARS, SUPER-NOVAS, NEBULAS, GALAXIES, BLACK HOLES, ETC.). And God saw that they were good. And there was an afternoon and a morning, the fourth day. And God said, let's do man to our image (THAT WAY, LIKE THE CHIMPS, and WITH OUTRAGEOUS RESEMBLANCES)

A version of the genesis, such as the above, was all that was needed to have God's existence proved with an absolute certainty.

However, the original version, deserves the following comments:

a   And God saw that it was good. Did not know God that whatever he created was extremely good?

b   And God said: Let's do man at our image. Now, the Catholic Church, approves Evolution, which contradicts the affirmation of the Genesis.

c   Have control and domain all over the land (to its total destruction, as we are close to achieve?)

d   He created the male and the female, from dust; or the woman from Adam's rib, decide believers, which one is the one that you believe?

e   Did he bless them?, it appears to be exactly the opposite. Regarding marriage, it did not "stick" either.

f   Multiply and occupy all land. Until we manage to destroy ourselves by over population, showing less intelligence than bacteria?

g   Why would he proceeded checking, day by day his work, as if he was uncertain of the results? Could he not create everything, by a single stroke?

h   Why did he rest the seventh day, does he get tired?

i   How about the creations of the millions of different microbes, bacterium, archea and parasites, without forgetting the virus, those animals appear to be God's favorites by the millions, even much more that the supposed God's creature? Nevertheless, the bible does not have a day mentioned for the creation for all of these nasty creatures. Seems to be, that God gave not importance to any of them, but surely, for all those animals, they certainly play an extremely important role, simply because all the damage they may cause!

In fact, in relation to the previous point d-.), the version that Eve came into being of Adam's rib is not even false in principle, rather the aforementioned fantasy does not even stick to the embryonic reality, given that we now know that all human fetus, basic and tentatively are feminine and the determination of the definite sex is postponed for a later moment. This is evident when examining the male body, which has nipples, the ones that are in no need for any moment of his life (this has been detailed previously).

What may have happened? Maybe God forgot to reveal the above deadly episode i-.), which may have happened the same day that he created all other animals or in the day that he created

Adam (and Eve). And in relation to Noah, he was supposed to have recollected said uncountable harmful sorts, not missing a single one. You see, he needed an electron microscope for an impossible to realize task. How do the creationists or the faithful of the *intelligent design* reply to these questions? Was it an oversight, or God required one additional day for the especial creation of that diabolical objective? Could he really had that objective in mind? But, which beneficial creator being can come up with the idea, of creating trillions of unicellular animals and even – beings not even living creatures– visible viruses only through an electron microscope, with an incomprehensible and rotund possible advantage to damage and kill, every animal and plant. For which reason, does this divinity favors this completely out of all proportion, microorganism universe? This action, is to me, one of my principal arguments against God's existence. If the reader wants to delve into this subject, I recommend to read Carl Zimmer's book; *Parasite Rex,* in order to appreciate the depth of this unnecessary and absurd problem (in a good design). Yes, I now that bacteria are indispensable for the digestion of food, but even these could be eliminated, counting on an intelligent proposal.

And in the last analysis: <u>*Homo sapiens, resulted the worst parasite that has had this planet, and this, with express divine indication.*</u>

Why it proved to be unthinkable for Jesus to conceive, at least one parabola, in which he could eliminate all (or at least, some) of the *mysteries* presented in the Bible. At least one that someday would give an *impressive* revelation that could prove to be truth. A revelation that could not leave behind any doubt about God's existence. Why *faith* is forced to all captive believers, and it is absolutely indispensable for the church? *Because, that way they control them, and accumulate immense wealth.*

But imagine, that Jesus gathers together his disciples (especially, the Greek thinkers above mentioned) and says to them: "See the firmament, can you observe its immensity? In truth, I say to you that a day (he could be much more specific!) will come, when I will send to earth Edwin Hubble (and to his important assistant Milton Humason), who will show the inhabitants of the earth, the true dimensions of the firmament, which it *is spreading out very fast,* and in that remote time, the firmament will be called: universe or cosmos (a more adequate name). This *mystery,* that you do not understand now, will be the irrefutable proof of my existence, because it is a true prophecy, that I am revealing to you, close to two thousands year in advance. This would have been a wonderful opportunity to answer Bertrand Russell, who express not believing in God, because there is not enough proof. In effect, there is not, but within this book (and tens of other books) there is an enormous quantities of proofs of God's nonexistence. I am going to afford, not to agree with so distinguished philosopher. I believe that a great quantity of proofs exist, <u>*but against*</u> God's existence, for me, other very conclusive, is the following; if we consider true, that the Deluxe chimp is the more important work of the creation, being this created to image and God's similarity. If this is the best *design,* that God can create, it would be a very mediocre designer, due to some worthy deficiencies, which contrasts with God's attributes.

Or to propose something closer to the *epoch of salvation;* Democritus, who lived four centuries before Christ, and he "baptized" the *atom* (that means *indivisible* in Greek), the smaller part of matter. Simply, Christ *may have revealed the mystery;*

that Democritus was wrong, and that the atom was divisible, with enormous difficulty, but divisible. He may have predicted that two thousand years afterwards, he would send Ernest Rutherford and Robert Oppenheimer (among others), to demonstrate it. Why was it impossible to accomplish?

The *Creed* prayer, −asks for blessings−, for the holy Catholic church. If something is not holy, it is the church. In Spanish, a prayer says literally: "saint mother church". This solicitous sentence begs for blessings for the church. Very understandable. But mentioning: "mother"? It is explained as: "God's children are generated within her breast, and that way we feed our spirituality". That is; like Jesus, also fatherless? It is evident that the *mother* concept that the church utilizes is very superficial. This term requires a 100% biological father necessarily. It is most probable that once the great quantity of virgins were accepted by the Catholics' approval, (for the church single mothers), the *mother concept* came up, with the idea of attaching it to the church. Talking about virgins, is it logic and realistic that a great quantity of them exist? Was it not enough with only one? The most important Mexican virgin is: the "Virgin of Guadalupe". Her anniversary is December 12, and gathers close to eight million believers, that come from almost everywhere of the Mexican Republic, at her large church (Basilica de Guadalupe). A good part of these believers walk all night long (fanatics), and a considerable part finishes the trajectory in their knees (super fanatics). There is not, another religious festivity that attracts, not even remotely, such catholic mass. Is it logic, or at least reasonable, that the aforementioned Virgin of Guadalupe, or anyone else attract believers' hordes, in a great deal in bigger measure, than any celebration of Jesus? Is the virgin more important than Jesus? She is so, for a great deal of Mexican Catholics, they have not, perhaps, become aware of this awkward fact.

Continuing with the evaluation of the church being self-named *saint*, when the facts show exactly the opposite. That is a very curious epithet for the *holy* crusades, for example, or for the martyrdom of uncountable scientists or simple opponents. How can they name themselves belonging to a saint-like institution, for goodness' sake? In relation to Guadalupe's large Church, his *Abad*, the priest Gillermo Shulemburg, previously in its care, pronounced himself, after thirty two years of doubt, which he grew to the point of frank incredulity, about the appearing of the Virgin of Guadalupe. Some events are worth believing in, but not in others. Some religion. Now, if he did become an unbeliever, why did he not renounced, that instant? Why did he preserve his place ("job")? Evidently, for the immense amount of money that flows at the mentioned temple. Thus, his "appointment" should be called it by his real name: his "business".

Then; we can speak of the heads of the organized crime, friends of the Cardinal Posidas Campos, who was assassinated by the brothers Arellano Félix (he was protector and confessor of them). A note in this subject was published by the reporter Héctor A. González (atpalabra.com 2001-06-06).

And now the worst part: unending rosary of known pederasts. The unraveled cases would certainly be unlimited. The most recent, and the most dramatic was the committed by (but he was not convicted); the priest Marcial Maciel, founder of the overpoweringly successful order; *Legionaries of Christ*, much better known as: *Millionaires of Christ*. This audacious present criminal, under protection of the high hierarchy of the church, especially of the Vicar of Christ: Juan Pablo II, was able to escape to the least punishment. In spite of his victims' multiple accusations, he never was taken into prison, his maximum punishment was: to *retreat to the private life* when he was already an octogenarian. Over fifty pederast's years finished with total impunity. The most recent ones of his evildoings got released recently. This cretin jerk raped a sixteen years old girl, of whom a girl was born several years ago. It has been proven, that he had several wives and children (to whom he also raped!). Of course he caused a great damage to dozens, or rather, hundreds of children (LA ORDEN MALDITA – MACIEL – PEDERASTA Y DROGO), (CARMEN ARISTEGUI Y MARCIAL MACIEL). Now, a vital question: this unnamable creature, who took; the name of Christ for his order of; "*Legionarios of **Cristo**"*, how is it possible that Christ (God), never acted, in no sense avoided this unfortunate group foundation, when his name got at stake, and a criminal was going to utilize it, for such intentions? For Jesus's indication: "Let the children come close to, because the Kingdom of Heaven comes from the ones that are like these. Matt 5:13-1". He and other pederasts took advantage of said call? Because, so it seems that has happened. Was Christ not aware of the dreadful damage done in his name, or at least with his name. *Does it not becomes clear that God never acts?, for the simple reason that, who does not exist, evidently, cannot act.* What more proofs the believers need?

I feel offended, in the same way that Richard Dawkins feels offended, (I AM OFFENDED RICHARD DAWKINS) but besides, in this occasion, for an event, of cynical mockery, owed to the fact that Juan Pablo II has been canonized. Supposing, without conceding, that he would have accomplished *a miracle*, why did not himself dedicated to perform miracle after miracle, against the clock, to accomplish thousands of miracles by the cure of sick thousands of people? Why *a* miracle only? Why he did not accomplish, even one restoration of a member lost by an amputation? That one alone, would be a miracle to consider! Imagine it as live transmission!

This Pope concealed and protected during practically all his life to the great criminal Marcial Maciel – so much sins the one that holds the paw, as the one that kills the cow–, and now he has been canonized? What is this about? Here it is demonstrated again, that the church, to its higher level, is as corrupt as the politicians and governing body. I believe that Mexico is a paradise (only for the criminals, not so, for the citizens that behave adequately), since there are no culprits of absolutely anything here (unless, you are poor), almost every criminal is immaculate, in a country putrefied of injustice and corruption. If that is the way that the church "acquires" its saints, why not also canonize Maciel!?, that way, they would be able to have the saint-like devil. But what about the Catholics? Why don't they become very angry in front of such a farce and cynicism? I feel very offended, and with grief for these lambs, that allow themselves, get "guided" without presenting the least opposition, and/or interrogation. A few months ago, that excellent and brave journalist Carmen Aristegui, interviewed some of the children born to Maciel's wives, and she has just published a book about this despicable individual's crimes (MARCIAL MACIEL, A CRIMINAL'S HISTORY), and the answer of the Catholic church is to beatify the protective accomplice?

Speaking of characters of evil doing, especially because it was investigated and was uncovered by Mr. Hitchens, and he calls her: "Hell's Angel". Here follow a few of the wrong doings of this character; she was found to have several checking accounts, one of them having more than fifty million dollars (outside of India, due to problematic tax laws). The money was utilized to build monasteries, not hospitals. She prepared patients for a good death, instead of a good life, since suffering is well seen by God. She was against divorce, except when Princess Diane did it, then Mother Theresa sent congratulations to said aristocrat. She was catapulted to fame when visiting a dark place, and a photographer decided to try a brand new film that was developed by Kodak, to utilize a very small amount of light. In effect, the film was great in that circumstances, so much so, that *a miracle* was proclaimed. Why are all modern miracles of so much low profile? Why not another stopping of the sun (the writers of the bible should have meant "earth" instead), or a similar feat? Simply because no real miracles had ever existed, exist now, or will ever exist. Pope John Paul II hurriedly canonized her, and I do not feel like writing about religious icons any longer. They are disgusting

The Mexican Cardinal, Norverto Riberas, who also proved to be protective of another pederast priest, Nicolas Aguilar, requested some time ago, protection to Mexico City's Regent, when people threatened him to death, when they became furiously angry. Didn't the cardinal know that, the founder of his religion (his boss) refused to ask protection for himself when he was unjustly accused? An action that probably would have avoided a cruel torture and death. Doesn't he knows also that becoming a martyr, possibly the principal of the religious positions, that he could be compensated by enjoying God's view, for all eternity? If he himself, is not convinced, about this act of faith, by self-example, why the Catholic community does not challenge his behavior?

The bishop of Ecatepec, has been and he is, another priest that likes very much luxury life. He is multimillionaires' friend, plays golf, and attends and performs at the more important social events. Some time ago, a federal judge, had filled for his arrest for indications of fraud, since the famous parish priest simulated a loan of 130 million dollars. Another little jewel of the "*saint-like mother* church! I mention, one of the several newspaper reports (La Jornada): "Onésimo Cepeda goes out, the factic power pastor" by Bernardo Barranco V. (Wednesday May 9, 2012), where his insipid and servile life is detailed. And how about the murky papal nuncio Prygione, whose track record frightens, *direct assignment from the Vatican.*

But to be fair, they have undoubtedly existed, and exist priests that behave as they are supposed to. Not too long ago, the news of the death of Zamuel Ruiz, bishop of San Cristobal de la Casas, Chiapas, who really helped the natives and in general to the unprotected practicing the: *Theology of the Liberation,* that was blocked by the Vatican (provides no money).

Almost with certainty the pederasts' number is immense and their protection and status from the church is guaranteed. As Darrell W. Ray explains in his book: *The God Virus*; the "vectors" (priests) are hard and expensive to acquire, and therefore they must be protected against any accusation.

Question; from where in hell, did the Catholic Church obtained the absurd and practically impossible to obey rule, that priests must remain celibate? Presumption (reality); the married priests, would need money to maintain their families, money that it ensues from accumulating in the church's safes. This *absolute unnatural restriction* has caused, among other terrible things; hordes of pederasts priests, but that is not important; the church and politicians will protect each other, meanwhile, Catholics will remain being *willingly* ignorant of such despicable facts, and they will keep on helping, and attending services at their saint-like mother church, as if nothing had happened. The important thing is: the schools and universities started by Maciel provide millions of dollars. When I asked a very religious person regarding her opinion about Maciel's crimes, her answer literally was that: "she preferred not to think". What are you tell me?

If you read about scientific subjects, you will, in all probability have read the term *Polymath*, and will certainly know that it refers to a person, that has very extensive and profound knowledge, about several disciplines. Do you happen to know some polymath, in person? Is he your friend? The answer to both questions is probably no, well then, I was pleased to know, as a friend, and from whom I learned very much. Following; I am going to take the opportunity to tell the reader a truthful interesting, and amenable history related to his multiple and extraordinary abilities. This story has a relation with this book, because refers to a religious issue at the end of his life. To this friend extremely special, I will call him Gonzalo Gonzalves. I first met Gonzalo at the University, being both students of engineering. As a student he was quite mediocre (but also Einstein, was a bad student), in one occasion the grade that he obtained in mathematics was less than 1 (in a scale from 0 to 10) and if I remember correctly, he never graduated. But, it is necessary to remember that, for example; Bill Gates and Steve Jobs also were dropouts, so not having graduated, does not tell anything, about your future. A noteworthy act, very irrational, that he performed was that, to prove that he could concentrate 100 % in spite of great pain, he maintained a lit match in his hand's palm, while solving a differential equation. Such feat, easily could have damaged permanently his hand, but fortunately he could recover. Gonzalo had a great quantity of friends that appreciated him, and they admired him, and also those who gathered in his home very frequently, far into the night. We would carry all kinds of devices in order that he would fix them for us, that would become fixed somehow rapidly (the waiting line was quite long), unless he needed spare parts. In particular, he liked to fix new technology apparatuses, unknown to him, but after a brief revision, he proceeded to take them apart, to fix them and then he proceeded to explain to us: both the theory and how and why, it worked. He, of course, had his preferred brands, specifically for their quality and technology, and of course, (almost) all friends proceeded to buy the recommended products, if we needed them. For example: Renaul better than BW, English amplifier Leack (tubes, of course) and working at UNIBAC a great deal better than IVM.

I am going to comment, of what I know that Gonzalo knew in detail in theory and in practice.

He could fix, practically any clock. He could fix any electric and electronic appliance. He could perform mayor repairs and tune up automobile engines. He could open locks and combination safes. He had a telescope and some knowledge in astronomy. Some other abilities that I no longer recall.

In one occasion, my automobile Renaul 8, was hit from the back, a great impact that unbalanced the chassis. Gonzalo, at that time, had conditioned his house's garage like a little workshop, which is why I attended for his help, in that epoch of our lives. Where he learned mechanics and body shop, I haven't the faintest idea, but in all probability he was self-educated, because you could bet that he never had worked at some workshop, since he had sufficient means and lived in a very nice neighborhood. Needless to say, the vehicle had been repaired perfectly.

His theoretic and practical knowledge was shared without selfishness, but rather, with great enjoyment at his house. He was a professor at the same school I also attended, in charge of, the physics laboratory for several years. Thus, he was completely qualified knowing all of the different areas belonging to physics, for secondary and preparatory levels. I do not know what he learned about Relativity and Quantic theories, but I imagine that he knew quite a bit of both.

In those days, one day I talked seriously to Gonzalo, and I recommended the following; Gonzalo, you should go to the U. S. and start working for the company that you choose, getting the best possible job, but it does not have great importance, in the beginning. Soon an opportunity will come, for example; your boss's car breaks down; you will offer yourself to fix it. Perhaps soon, to somebody you know, his TV breaks down, which you will offer yourself to fix. Perhaps to someone, a clock breaks down that you also fix. Soon your varied and multiple knowledge and abilities arrive to top management's ears and you are called and be asked what type of laboratory you wish to run. Because, of course, that there are many polymath in the U.S., but they are just too much theoretical but not theoretical and *practical* like in your case. But Gonzalo never took my suggestion seriously.

Eventually Gonzalo was hired by Unibac where he learned programming, and I understand that he got to be manager of software *and* hardware since he could solve problems of programming (the operating system), as well as fixing hardware, that is the whole computer, to be necessary. Being myself working within the computation industry, that one is the only one case that I knew, of a manager of both areas in simultaneous form. Being very happy Gonzalo at the aforementioned company and with his work, certain day he suffered a very severe heart attack that he survived, but never was able to recover completely. And here it is, where the religious situation appears. Given that Gonzalo had studied in a school run by Jesuits, he had also an *indelible mark*. I never had the furthest impression that he was a practicing Catholic, because he was so close to science, the odds are that he would be an agnostic, at least. However, since that event, he dedicated himself to the study of the Bible, period. And only in very rare occasion we could go back to see him.

Could it be: *sudden fear to death* that led him and his wife to such drastic change? That is, religion became his crutch in order for him to continue limping for life. I still continue to miss and think about him frequently.

Given that the first part of this book, perhaps I should have named it: *The Unending Questions (unanswered),* the following question is the one that a believer of any religion should ask himself; of the hundreds of religions that have existed (A SHORT LIST OF GODS), for what happy, lucky and really peculiar reason, would the religion each believer chooses to follow, could be the one true and only? (RICHARD DAWKINS - WHAT IF YOU'RE WRONG) (I'VE HAVE CONVERTED TO EVERY RELIGION, JUST IN CASE)? Because if so happens that, if one is not born in such religion, or convert to it, one will go to hell, independently of that if you lived like a saint, or quite the contrary (AN ATHEIST MEETS GOD).

The United States is sick of *religionitis*. Like a very serious contagious disease, the U.S. in particular (as well, as the rest of the planet) is congested with an impressive number of religions, that by only seeing the size of its temples and cathedrals, one can estimate the large sum of money, that they recollect. You can get a good picture, if you visualize themselves, like very capable companies, in guiding the people with need of crutches. Priests, cures, shepherds, rabbis, or as they may call themselves, are highly trained to convince, the ones that have not gotten worried in getting ready to fend off, this very clever *businessmen's* type. They, incredibly, convince the parishioners *attacked by faith*, of that immense religions list; *that,* such, in particular, is the one that is necessary to practice. Incredibly, they *put the people on*, because they have not been in contact with the scientific method. They have not read evolution. They have not read the *BALONEY DETECTION KIT*, by Carl Sagan. They have not read some scientific book(s). Or even worse, they have perhaps read scientific important literature, but they have been unable to understand its importance, truth and consequences. Religions, are the only businesses, where people give money which contradicts the saying:" There is no free lunch". For the churches, you have it, and excessively. In reality, the parishioners give great quantities of money as a present and they get in return; the *force of faith*, that translated it means: *you have in your soul an immense sense of guilt, which can amend itself with charity (money)*, with which they create absurd belief, and they prepare the believers, in order that, they do not believe all of the important scientific theories, based in overpowering proof (such as evolution). The idea (need) to write this paragraph happened during a recent journey to New York. At the small town, where I was staying, (similar to the majority of the towns), on Main street, there were five churches in a terrain of only three streets. Two belonged to acknowledged religions, and the others had the rarest imaginable names. How do these new denominations manage to subsist? How do the shepherds (or whatever they call themselves) achieve and get hold of their followers? Only by being excellent businessmen, experts in marketing, no doubt about it. When I saw this scheme, immediately it came to my mind, the computer company where I worked. Anywhere that this company established itself, immediately, the competition itself (Hewlet Pakard, CBC, UniBac, etc.), would follow and established themselves very close by. The same thing happens when General Motores finds its place at some building, soon the agglomerate of the rest of the automotive get around. This is a strategy of marketing that has demonstrated its efficacy. That way, the churches of *all believes* have copied it. What's been said: the priests know their business well.

The disastrous worldly situation, in spite of millions of daily prayers and of religious services of numerous religions offer is deep proof that: *In God we trust* (In God we are confident) that appears in the dollar bills, produce void results (THE BEST OPTICAL ILLUSION IN THE WORLD). What definitely it has resulted prophetic, is the bald eagle with the 13 arrows that symbolize war. Because, if in something they are ultra-expert and they are ultra-prepared is in wars, and they are ready for a true: *war of the galaxies.* I suggest to the U.S. government emphatically, that they should check its bills design, although I understand that hardly, it would be taken seriously, specifically that; *In God We Trust*, should be changed to *In Science We Trust*, counting of course, that a *wise utilization* of this may be achieved. Remember that, according to the genesis, the Deluxe chimps were expelled from paradise because they ate from the *tree of knowledge* of right and wrong. What else does it takes to prove and demonstrate, that to trust in God, has not benefit, will give no use ever to our planet, and a lot less to the personal level, but quite the contrary.

Thus, had it not been exclusively due to science, we Deluxe chimps would live on at caves, or almost. (A MUST SEE FOR A CREATIONIST).

How about the very tenacious visitors of Jehovah's witnesses, continuously ringing in my house, trying to convince me?… if they only knew what type of books I write! But I never will try to convince, not even one of them, of the least doubt on his/her beliefs, because I know that it is totally useless, and because I, as well as, the immense majority of the atheistic community, we are not proselytizing, going from house to house, gathering in meetings, searching to change forms to think, for mistaken that they may be, and looking for followers on what to believe, or rather, on what not to believe.

I am not interested at all, or find some kind of pleasure, when insulting Homo sapiens. I just say, what it has to be said, about the Deluxe chimp. But, if the above-mentioned religious groups communicate that: *man came into being as image and God's similarity,* and besides they spread it out in public, *especially at the schools, instead of the truth of evolution,* I believe that it is necessary to make science known and do something. For God's sake! Any believer observe yourself naked, in front of a mirror. Do you see, anything remotely related to God's image, or do you see an animal's image, almost just like every mammal, especially, of course, chimps. For God's sake!, and if *besides,* they dare tell to the world, that *the universe was made for us*, in what type of head that fits in, let's be reasonable.

At the final part of this chapter, I will try to accomplish my last attempt to convert some creationists/intelligent design believers that may be reading this book, and still go on, *with firm beliefs like rocks.*

I encountered myself in the final revision of the book, when I came up with an analogy, that in the beginning it seemed nonsensical to me; let's see if I can argument it reasonably enough, if not so, I will simply discard it:

Let's suppose that we are told, or it was written in a sacred book (by Greek mathematicians, no fishermen almost surely illiterate) *that; it was not possible to demonstrate any mathematical theorem*, but as the largely known Grand Master Pythagoras: **a theorem had been revealed to them, and they had blind faith that it was true.** The equation that all of us learned at primary school:

$C^2 = A^2 + B^2$, which says: the square of the hypotenuse is equal to the sum of the squares of the sides of a triangle *for any right-angled triangle* (Catholicism). Now then, let's suppose that somebody finds *a single case that* this does not prove to be the case (Protestantism). The true mathematicians, at that point, loose their confidence (faith), in the aforementioned theorem. The least purists would say, strange thing! They would perhaps be able to think; OK, is not necessary to get worried, it has been found the only exception that exists. Said theorem would be feeble, but it would be able to ensue utilizing, but now with more care, another fault could be encountered, another exception. And it does happens, in several places, they find examples of situations where that equation do not hold preciseness (Evangelists, Methodists, Baptists, etc.). However, they follow the majority of the people that *do not think*, utilizing the mentioned theorem with absolute confidence (faith), knowing that the resulting calculations that they obtain, evidently prove to be somewhat erroneous. Worse still, there began to appear new *teachers* that begin to modify the theorem, that go from subtle variations as: ($C2 = A^2 + B^2 + 0,001$), to drastic changes (*for any type of triangle: Rectangle, isosceles and scalene*); (Islamism, Buddhism, Mormonism, etc.) In spite of the fact, that the original theorem was false, each accepted change, proved to be very much worse, actually, totally out of reality. They have appeared new big teachers, or rather, big phony's, right and left, whom nobody questions in the least.

The absurd of the absurd: the great majority of people, *keep on believing in the original theorem, **and in all its variants.*** (Catholicism, Judaism, Pentecostalism, Quakers, Unitarians, Universalists, Church United of Cristo, Adventists, Christians, Dravidians, Church of the Seventh-Day Adventist, Behaísmo., etc.) (I'VE HAVE CONVERTED TO EVERY RELIGION JUST IN CASE).

That analogy seemed very interesting to me, which is why I will not discard it. I believe that it presents a very good analogy with the approval of religions, but I fear myself, that the faithful, they may accept this example, but not the analogy (mathematics: yes, but religion: no).

I recommend emphatically to all Catholic, agnostic, atheist, and in general, to every person, and any person's family members that are about to die, to be careful, watchful of any priest or shepherd, present in the aforementioned moment. Priest are known of uncountable cases, where they are able to convince to donate (property and bank accounts), to their respective church (because of the fear to die), in order that God may forgive all his/her sins, and to go directly to heaven, instead of hell, where they will convert multitude of dreadful and eternal torments in reality. This is one of the principal means for obtaining the immense riches, that old and afraid elders give to new (and old) churches that have gotten to be so enormously rich and powerful.

FOUR

Other issues that God forgot

"Only two things are infinite: the universe and the human
stupidity, and I am not very sure about the first".

Albert Einstein

If in something we should look like *God's image,* it would
be necessarily and primarily in intelligence, given that this
faculty is the one that separates us from all the other animals,
although only in grade, but not in type. Frankly, I cannot imagine
God deciding to become an ape. And we are precisely in this area
in where the Deluxe chimp, more and more radically has gotten
away from exercising the aforementioned faculty.

The people that have lived in the XX and XXI centuries have
had an enormous luck, especially the ones that can rely on their
capacity of amazement, as well as, the ones that are interested
in knowing the scientific advances, most of all, when these are
headed for the well-being of humanity. But it so happens that,
for most people, the most trivial imaginable things appeal to
them. They are extremely interested, in knowing if a famous star
self-pronounces *homo, or* if a famous singer appeared naked. Just
watch what appears when opening several pages in the Web, and in
the facades of almost any magazine.

Thus, the knowledge of the genome of many animals,
especially, −the human genome−, the space adventure, the

electronic wonders like; the Internet, the Ipod, etc., shows the fact that, the Deluxe chimp has an intellect capable for really incredible, unsuspected and unpredictable complex advance. But the acquaring of all this knowledge has been extremely slow, and at times, harmful, traumatic and even mortal for groups of tens (hundreds?) of scientists during the middle ages, with Galileo, and even worse still, for Giordano Bruno, by the Catholic church. That the Inquisition was called "Santa" (holy) to name that institution; only has occurred to the Catholic Church. What a different situation it would have been if God (if existed), like a loving human father, that really love his children, would show himself continuously. That father, would make his best effort to leave the best prepared his children, in order for whatever life presented itself. Here, I am supposing that the aforementioned father (or mother), is an educated man and thus, he is able to pass that education to his children. I do not ask much, I am not suggesting that God *should send us off to the world* with Ph. D's or even Master's degrees, but I am suggesting that, by no means, we should have not been kicked out of paradise, as I mention in another part of the book, empty-handed without a minimum of some type of help, in order that, we had not wasted ten thousand or so years, catching up with the level of present-day knowledge.

Because, everything seems to indicate that we, Deluxe chimps, are approaching tremendously quickly the end of our civilization (at least, as we know it). We have created so many and so formidable problems, that we found ourselves in *an unprecedented predicament,* that according to uncountable scientific associations, scientists and writers, and by our daily experience, everything seems to fit the predictions and mathematical models that they are telling us; I am totally convinced, but I hope that they (and I) be dead wrong. I ask myself: how is it possible that God, seeing the disaster that we have done of this planet, *does not move a finger*, what is he waiting for? In Miguel Angel's famous painting in the Sistine chapel, where God's finger almost touches the finger of man. That "almost" touching is prevalent. Could not God finally, in reality, *make contact with* his image, in order to see, if that way we could improve the human conduct radically? Could he not also accomplish a *revelation* to the Pope and give a "solution" to the mentioned predicament? If is not now, when could it be, that is more demanding? Did God made a revelation regarding Virgin Mary's assumption, something totally irrelevant and false, and he does not reveal how to save the planet from his *image,* the – Deluxe chimp –, is it possible that God does not know how to accommodate priorities, regarding what and when to reveal something?

If we came into being as God's image and similarity, why we obtained our body and supposedly our soul and there the similitude stops. Why God did not accomplish *transference* of some love to our neighbors, that is, to the generations that will follow ours, among other things. With respect to the avarice that poisons the majority of humans, could not Jesus share his humility with us? Seems to be that free will took precedence in his teachings, which were only theoretical and by example, but not transmitted to our bodies so that we "inherited" his behavior. That is, at least, for me, a bad design.

Being God the architect par excellence, the engineer par excellence, the mathematician par excellence and the artist par excellence, in other words, the divine Leonardo Da Vinci: why did he not transferred all, or some invaluable capabilities (to human level, of course) to his favorite creature? What is the purpose to create such complex brain with billion of nerve cells, with ten thousand connections, and many with close to fifty thousand, that is, *almost for certain, the most complicated "appliance" of the universe in terms of computation,* that *is to say: the hardware?*

What I will refer to, is a process of mental multi-tasks, in addition to the corporal control. Given the enormous complexity of our brain, one related comment is that even Einstein only occupied a small percentage of his capability, that unused surplus of not utilized resource, could be useful to comply with the function above described. In conclusion: the *operating system* of the Deluxe chimp when is born, supposedly created (according to the Bible) to God's image occupies: zero Terabytes, zero Gigabytes, zero Megabytes, zero K bytes and without exaggerating zero *operating* bits. Only would be on, the bits needed to survive, like any other animal. That is, his/her Operating System is totally blank. Or should I say, full of zeroes? And, if when we were born, we did not come already with the desired and required software, we will never have it. The creation's most complex being was half-designed? Hardware without software?

Thus, if the *design* of the Deluxe chimp, was the best design that he was able to create, taken as his image, frankly *that* God, does not generate in myself the least credibility. Evidently, I would believe in a God that *really* complies with the attributes that I have mention previously, deducting certainly, and all the mysteries and in short, the Bible. That God, I am certain, would of have taken care of leaving behind evident certainty of his existence. In fact, there would not even be need to believe, *his existence would really be evident.*

Suggestions for a new design in a parallel universe, and achieved intervening a thinking God, not a Tlaloc. At the risk of proving to be repetitive, the following are only some desirable characteristics in the cosmos:

A lot bigger human life span to maximum capability, if not eternal

Foodstuff that assimilates entirely, without any waste (forget the large intestine and urine)

Easy replacement of living parts

Less Homo (testosterone) and a lot more sapiens (applied intelligence)

Energy not contaminant unlimited or at least enough for some milenia

Pain expressed on a totally different way

Non-existent avarice

Quality raw living material, or perhaps living matter better thought

Mental ubiquity

Non-existent entropy

A universe designed, with life in mind, without dangers

Nothing of dust, galaxies formed of another clean substance

No sweat

No diseases, that is: zero virus, bacteria and parasites of any type

Neither depredators, nor need for agriculture

Operation and User's Manual of the universe and its components

Evident and corroborative proof of God's existence

Money impossible from being invented

If there is some especial being, that it would not be an evolution from an ape, I am sure, there are much better options

Etc.

FIVE

Perennial wrongdoing in the Deluxe chimp by its design

"Man is a filthy and nasty creature."

Carlos Tejeda

Undoubtedly, the wrongdoings of the Deluxe chimp have existed from ancestral times. It is read in the Bible that Cain killed his brother Abel. Cain was the first-born son of Adam and Eve and the first born human out of paradise. That way; Adam and Eve, they failed to God, because they disobeyed him, and for that reason they were thrown off paradise. Coming to the point: Adam and Eve did not obey God. Their son kills his brother. That is: _the first three humans failed God miserably._ Frankly: is this a good design?

Does this failure not say absolutely anything to the priests and to the faithful? In other words, an "F" to God in design, Lucifer three victories, equivalents to an "A". If we add Lucifer's design, who also failed God, the scoreboard shows: four very bad designs by God, with an "F" grade and Lucifer retains his "A" with four victories. I imagine that the disobedient and arrogant angel's case, excuses him by the church, by the free will, that also has to have been bestowed it in his creatures upon even his more favorite's creatures, than the Deluxe chimp, because _they were created with_ eternal existence. As I commented in a previous chapter, if the excuse is *free will,* which becomes very useful, for freeing God from all responsibility, and that way the accused become angels and humans of all of the evils that existed, exist and they will exist on earth (and in heaven), which shows plenty of bad designing.

It is said, and I have read, that the aforementioned free will, serves us well, because if we could not make mistakes, there would be no progress. I agree partially with this reasoning, but I do not agree, that free will to *be total*, without absolutely no maximum check point. I compare this absolute freedom, to any physical process that can destroy itself (run away situation), that can happen frequently.

SIX

Arguments against this book

Common errors of logic and rhetoric.

Ad hominem: attacking the arguer instead of the argument

My original manuscript: *Deluxe chimp,* loaned to my two friends, in order that, they gave out their opinion to me, consisted of the four first chapters of this book plus others, that present the terrible predicament that is facing Homo sapiens, related to the very close future pertaining to; Global Warming, Peak Oil, Water Wars, and diminishing nonrenewable resources that are running out. All of these directly blamed to overpopulation.

In the above mentioned manuscript, I proposed a method for the substantial improvement of intelligence that possibly could be able to reduce the size of the dreaded announced possible catastrophe that is to be taken with seriousness, urgency and globalization. Based on the answer (so negative), that I received from the two first readers, I made the decision that the religious material, should necessarily be presented in another book (this one). One of them (this book) would treat the religious issue and another book whose title is, as said above; Deluxe chimp, would treat the above-mentioned themes, reducing the mentioning of religious issues. The reason for this change is evident. The religious issue deviates any possibility of impartial rational analysis. Following, I will narrate the details that pulled over such change. In truth, I am very grateful with my two friends, who in the nick of time (before the original book's publication) and with a totally different intention, they helped me indirectly to separate the above issues, to be presented in two books, rather than in only one.

Hopefully, you have read the text carefully, each and every one of the arguments, and most of all, the great quantity of questions that I ask myself, and the ones that I leave in the air, the *impartial* reader will be able to appreciate the analysis that I do, to the emails that I received from my extremely believing and devotee friend. The reason to present such emails, is that you are shown a very clear distortion, and its missing capability of cold and intelligent analysis, when the theme to try is religion, it is an issue that cannot be treated *even with a rose's petal.* The three textual emails; I will present them one by one, followed by my logical dissection. The sentences with cursive writing suggest that the aforementioned portion, will be the one that I will examine, in relation to its applicability, in relation to what is written by me in this book. Granted that the comments expressed (or the ones that were absent to express) by my believing friend are anonymous and besides, anyway, I suppose that in this case also the reply right exists:

Email 1 (sent by my friend)

Until now, everything fine, I read all the way through the introduction of the book, and I had problems to stop. It is of very interesting truth, your English is outstanding and the book, until now really good. Congratulations, I will keep on reading it as soon as I get to my house.

Email 1 (analyzed by myself)

Analysis of the mail 1: You consider the <u>introduction of the very interesting book</u> and in general even happiness splits the book, really good. You say that you found it difficult to stop and then getting to your house you are going to go on with the reading. If you like it, really I am thankful to you.

The copy that he received was in English because originally it seemed to me that, more English readers exist, until I found out about, what problematical is the finding of editors in the U.S. (until I found Palibrio).

Email 2 (sent by my friend)

I have just finished the thorough reading of your book. Your command of the English language, <u>*the book* </u>is incredible <u>*you are doing very well, certainly interesting and amusing.* </u>Of course it contain themes that not only you dominate, as music, especially Jazz, mathematics, etc. There are others issues like evolution that one perceives that you went into them carefully and with excellent bibliography and a complete knowledge and understanding I can see what you write of, based, in a serious study of the themes. <u>*However, when you write on God, in my opinion it is a complete failure. I mean what, it is that in this concrete subject, it has a base more in rage than in the reason, it seems to me, really. And I am sorry, but that is the way that I felt in the time that I read all about God, religion and the introduction of the related material.*</u>

<u>*Your radicalism on this theme appears very clearly to the reader*</u>, without a doubt. However, I have liked very much the part when you write about the school you attended and the father Carlos Fernandez Moreno. <u>*It does not become a wonder that you were called the bad guy.* </u>And as you mention getting baptized that way

because in that epoch you were a mischievous child and certainly you used not to put absolutely no attention during his religion class and, therefore, you did not learn anything about God and Christian's religion. You challenged the fact that to assist every day to mass is radical. Not to mention your grandmother, who assisted to three consecutive masse daily if not more was totally crazy and therefore nonsense, even irrational, and you could not understand it. Also you affirm that your mother was live suffering testimony afflicted in her face (your personal interpretation, probably erroneously) when returning from church.

The fact that religion is something that does not worry you, so you decided, to avoid it altogether. Later in your life, you had rationalized more deeply on it and you challenged facts like right and wrong, that is, for example the insects that sting the people and diseases infect to innocent people (indeed, mosquitos are the evolution's product, not so?) And you blame God for it. All your thought has a base, according to understanding and perception (perhaps mistakenly, one more time) in received signs delivered you at tender age of life. Probably bad signs that turned you into an atheist. Are you to blame? Is it your fault? Nobody's fault? I don't know, but the problem is that I am a believer and I attend mass every day, well then we are in opposed, difficult positions to come to an agreement between you and me in this so important subject and I feel worried by the fact that you consider an atheist and you say it with so much frankness, so convinced.

When I read that part specifically, I sensed that you were not the writer, but next I gave myself account that yes, this was my long-life friend affirming it in a very serious way. Perhaps, a slender hope is, that you do consider the fact that can exist an "Absolut" where order must exist and everything else can be related to him. Otherwise it is all chaos. There is some chaos without a doubt, but also order, the stars and planets would otherwise collapse and possibly may not take shape, the universe would not exist. The universe is a careful planning's product and it supposes an intelligent being behind, in my conception. But it clear perception is relative, true? Perhaps there are so many perceptions as people or intelligent creatures in the universe exist. And it is your perception all about God once this book was thought about, but there are others.

Email 2 (examined by myself)

1."The book is very well written, certainly interesting and amusing".

That is, he considers it a book of quality, in everything that can refer to a good book.

2. "However, when you write on God, in my opinion it is a complete failure. What I mean, is that in this concrete subject, it has a base more in rage than in the reason, it seems to me, really. And I am sorry, but the way that I felt in the meantime while reading all about God, religion and the introduction of the related material.

It is, therefore, a very good book, except if I mention anything about God and/or religion. In that issue, the book, it is a complete failure, that is, I do not have the minimal knowledge, and I am 100% mistaken. Except in the paragraph where; "I express that I Am offended" (that it is not the same thing as to have rage), where I ask inconvenient questions, however much I check about what I wrote, I do not find the minor sign of rage, and I find reason in each line, because the majority of the text consists of questions, or else the fact that they were supposed to have considered for a good designer consists in suggestions, nothing else. Now, when I write about garbage such as Marcial Maciel (and similar), of course that makes me very angry, I cannot stand still and quiet, as you and the rest of Catholics do!

Also I present a variety of situations that, to have made good use of, the issue of proof of God's existence would have been resolved, beyond the shadow of a doubt.

"And I am sorry, but it is the way that I felt exactly" *Aha*!: Here is the problem. **I did not write the book, in order that the people feel, but in order that the people think.** The unconscious betrayed you. One of the principal problems of religions is that one precisely, that, even intelligent people, makes it impossible to consider, they go by what *they feel*.

You have a base more in rage than in the reason, besides, according to the scientific argument, if we considered the Baloney Detection kit, it shows to be an attack; ad hominem, that is, attack the man, not the argument.

That is what happens in this case exactly. Not one of the tens of arguments that I present in the book, are refuted, not even mentioned.

3. Your radical approach on this theme appears very clearly to the reader,

Without a doubt, if for radical approach, is to be understood that I examine the treated concept in depth, and I say all that I have to say with firmness, and with the adequate words, really, in that sense, I am very radical.

4. *However, I have liked very much the part when you write about the school you attended and the father Carlos Fernandez Moreno. It is not a strange thing that you were named the "bad guy". And as you mention getting baptized that way because in that epoch, because you were a mischievous child.*

To me, it is strange that a neat Jesuit had baptized myself a bad guy, a mischievous child (a little normal boy), for the simple reason that, my classroom mates, is common knowledge that they can become very mocking and cruel and they can make life impossible. Fortunately, this was not my case, – I could not care less –, that they try to make fun of me, but for other child, may have been a very nasty situation.

5. And *certainly you used to put absolutely no attention in his classrooms of religion* and, *therefore, you did not learn anything about God and of the Christian religion.* Rotund affirmations, I believe: "**Certainly**", putting "**absolutely**" **no attention,** you **"did not learn anything"**. These three convincing asseverations in a single paragraph; *to that, I call radicalism!* I learned what they taught me, because there were examinations, I had to study and besides back then, I did not have the faintest idea of doubt in relation to religion, only became very rare mysteries. Mentioning in my book God's attributes and the genesis, it is true that I have copied them, in order to have the complete and exact text, but of course, I remember, in general, the aforementioned information, although I may not recite it, to the letter. As from the above copied text, I present my dissertation, which, does not require for more *deep* knowledge of God. As my friend proposes; "You did not learn anything", granted that the majority offers doubts, questions and suggestions of the reason why the Homo sapiens design contains such and so many imperfections when God, if it should exist,

had to be able to realize a more intelligent design and with much better raw material (if it is that he needed one) of the best existent or created explicitly in the case of not existence, insuperable, or simply, as from nothingness.

6. As a *like little boy and as a teenager you challenged the fact of attending every day or even three times to mass, as your grandmother did it, for you, it was totally crazy and nonsense, even irrational, and you could not understand it.*

The questioning is being made now that I am writing the book and remembered the mentioned events, at that time, I did not mind if my grandmother wanted to sleep at the church. But right now, as an adult, I asses that I cannot understand such attitude, that has the very clear name of fanaticism, and this, in fact, is radicalism. In other words, religion acting in its normal form.

7. *Also you affirm that your mother suffered and testimony afflicted her face (your personal interpretation, probably erroneously) when returning from the church.*

I affirm it, because I lived it during all her life, always it was all the same, her intense suffering was not my interpretation. In order to verify it, anyone of my brothers and sisters can be asked with regard to this matter. Besides, it is very clear in the book, that **this happened inside of the church, not when returning from the church.** Because my friend *is feeling* too much, he is losing too much concentration. My interpretation (it was not interpretation, it was palpable reality), which,_*I was who lived it*_, he questions it, because really, according to his feelings, when I write about God,_**_EVERYTHING_**_, is a failure.

8. Thus since religion is something that does not worry you, you decided, to avoid it altogether. Later in your life, you had rationalized more deeply on it, you challenged facts like right and wrong, that is, for example: the insects that sting people and diseases infect to innocent people (indeed, mosquitos are the evolution's product, or not so?) And you blame God for it.

No doubt that I want to avoid religion by all means, even much more now, after checking, – your have *proven* me –, the terribly harm that comes out, for example, when reading my friend's email, very competent professional in computation and management, but you are not able to accomplish an impartial and quiet analysis, when the issue is religion. In relation to the mosquitos, I ask *ironically* in my book, that if God existed, he could of have designed the world without plagues, like for example mosquitos. But that is not *blaming* God, if I do not believe in him, how could I blame him?

9 All you're thinking is based, according to my understanding and perception (perhaps mistakenly, one more time) in received signals that you received at a tender age. Probably bad signals that turned you into an atheist. Was it your fault? Not your fault?, Someone *fault?*

From where does he concludes that all my thought is based on received signs delivered during my tender age. I indicated clearly that, although as a youth I had some doubts, after my mother's death, it is when I decided to become an atheist, how I say it in the book: Since my mother died (just short of 103 years of age), I leaved behind that (self-imposed) restriction. Then, I made the decision from turning not only agnostic, but to take the more deep position of atheist. This drastic change, I based in simple reasoning, evaluation of the scientific proof and the reading of several books, such a: *The Blind Watchmaker* and *The God Delusion* both of Richard Dawkins, *God is not Great of Christopher Hitchens*, and many others.

10. *I don't know, but the problem is that I am a believer and I attend mass every day, we are then in opposed sides, difficult positions to come to an agreement between you and me in this so important subject and I feel worried by the fact that you consider yourself an atheist and you say it with so much frankness, so convinced.*

Which problem? What coming to an agreement? Why are you worried because I am an atheist? Which is the problem with frankness and conviction?

11 When I read that specific part, I sensed that you were not who talked, but next, I realized that yes, it was my long-life friend affirming it, in a very serious way. Perhaps, there remains a slender hope.

Hope of what? Of course I affirm it in a very serious way, it's no joke. Convince me of what? Are you joking? I believed that you said that I affirmed it in a very serious way.

12. *You do not consider the fact that an Absolut must exist and everything else can be related to him.*

From where do you extract the idea, that an absolute **must exist***?* Exactly for what reason?". Until over a century ago, the great Newton's theory said : T*here must exist an Absolute time*, which Einstein refuted and demonstrated, not to be the case. You better would say there c*ould* be an Absolute, no more.

13. Otherwise, all would be chaos. There is some chaos without a doubt, but also order, the stars and planets would otherwise collapse and possibly may not take shape, the universe would not exist.

That is; a perfect God creates a chaotic universe but with some order, that is: chaotic order, something like: motionless movement? Don't you see this as a very weird reasoning? No, you don't.

14. The universe has a careful planning's and it supposes an intelligent being behind, in my conception. But clear perception is relative, true? Perhaps there are so many perceptions as people or intelligent creatures in the universe exist.

Correct, my view, as my book says, it is that the universe does not presuppose God's existence, enough theories explain the totally different cosmos mentioned as firmament in the Bible, do you remember? Tuned constants? That is what you call a totally inhospitable place for life, where we are witness of uncountable collisions that, at times, almost destroy and absolutely devastates all sort of heavenly bodies. Places where even the most beautiful galaxies collide and get distorted. Black holes, apparently in all galaxies where they absorb all that gets pass its event horizon, destroying it.

15. And it is your perception all about God once this book was thought about, but there are others.

Of course, there are others and ***my conclusion is that what you read in over sixty pages, you did not refute, specifically, not even one of my arguments.***

In conclusion: The evaluation of my book by my friend was contradictory (very good book in the first email and completely mistaken in the second email). The extremely poor contents of his second email merits a very strong reply, that I felt obligated to examine myself. I am absolutely certain that my friend would never read this book again, when it is published. Since his name does not appear in any part of the book, nobody will know to what friend I refer to. Finally, I decided not to send the above analysis to him, given that the only result would be the breaking of our friendship. Only a simple email was sent to him as follows:

Email 2 (sent to my friend)

I have the following comments to your previous email:

1. Granted that I believe to know you well, and to your religious dedication. I feared that my book could have turned out to be offensive to you. It gave me a lot of pleasure that you did not withdraw your friendship.

2. Certainly I was somewhat worried as how you would react to the anti-religious part of the book, but you focused, almost exclusively to this, which, for me, it is of little importance. The really important and worrisome, at least for me, it is the imminent global catastrophe (in this century) that is predicted to occur, that I mention in the book. In like manner, the proposed theme of the improvement of intelligence, you do not mention it, at all, that if it does not takes place fast, ample and global, or any other method, and I fail to see but very remote possibilities to succeed. We are elderly, but what about our children and grandchildren.

3. Curiously the fact that you focused *only in religion*, opened my eyes, as to that the anti-religious part is now a separate

book, just as I had it originally. Since I see that you were distracted and concentrated the attention in something extremely important to you that you deducted importance to the rest of the book, the most important part. Besides many people will not read the book, due to religious contents, apparently out of place, but actually, unfortunately, forms part of every civilization: religion.

4. That of course implicates to rewrite both books, but in reality it proved to be very valuable, thank you very much.

Thanks again and until later……..

From the other friend, that was to revise my manuscript, I never heard from him again, that was, two years ago.

SEVEN

Sanctified?, or damned be your kingdom

As Cristopher Hitchens said; "how religions poison everything", but I only am referring in this book to the religion that I was indoctrinated with, and of that myself never (not after my later teenager years), was I, a convinced believer. For several decades (probably much centuries, or even millennia), some of the pederasts have made themselves known, but they are never punished (with exemplary punishments!), neither by justice (?), nor by the Vatican, not even by the faithful! From where does comes the so brutal force that the religion have? It is absolutely amazing that, as far as I remember, no priest has been ever judged, and thus convicted of the thousands crimes against children, all over the world by Catholic priests. This impunity, evidently require, that these governments are corrupt, and do not protect their children (or older).

Almost all religions have as their principal characteristic the sacrifices. This cruel and ignorant act, invented thousands of years back, continue currently used in global form. In the particular case of Catholicism, its founder suffered it (according to the writings). But it proves to be vital to ask: taking into consideration the teachings of the Bible, millions of sacrifices are carried out daily by the Deluxe chimp. Which is the purpose of Homo sapiens?

Supposedly, to go to heaven (when lucky), but, which is purpose of the animals such as: chickens, pigs, cattle and several others? Because they are born *exclusively,* to get sacrificed (normally, with plenty of cruelty), in order to become the food of the Deluxe chimp, living very short lives in places in excess confined. What celestial father more benevolent!

Why was Jehovah so greedy purveying his favorite creatures? Without a doubt, the ten commandments tablet has certain value (the last seven), but anyway (with the tablet, or without it), any civilization that wanted to survive, sooner or later, it had to be able to find and exercise said basic standards of behavior, or they would not survive for a long time. Frankly, multiplication tables would have been much more useful, and the rest of our present-day basic, intermediate teaching, university, mastery, doctorates and post doctorates. As much as Homo sapiens has found it difficult to obtain this knowledge, even being the selected creature by God. And this knowledge to get a level 0 civilization, is as far as we have advanced.

Kardashov's scale is a method proposed in 1964 by the Russian astrophysicist to measure a civilization grade of technological advancement. He suggested three categories, the so-called type I, II and III, based in the quantity of usable energy that a civilization can utilize, which is incremented in an exponential manner. These types are also based in the grade of space colonization:

Civilization Type I: has been able to utilize all the energy his planet can produce. Civilization Type II: control and utilizes the energy of his solar system. Civilization Type III: control and utilizes the energy of his entire galaxy. Homo sapiens currently has attained .072, which suggests that we could advance to Civilization Type I; in some 100 to 200 years, and so forth (which given the predicament we are in, I doubted it very much). But, just imagine that God would have provided all that documented information, to Adam and Eve. Well, bad luck, that was not our case, expelled from paradise for being disobedient, but, at least, to grant his favorites creatures with a good-by present, for their survival and advance, was it really, too much to grant pardon of sins for such good loving and almighty father?

Why wait for a Babel Tower, where so much difference of idioms, would end up with a world inundated by different languages? Why only one favorite tribe, how about the rest of the world? A world with one idiom and besides the information given above mentioned, could have saved centuries and centuries of suffering, proof and error, and ignorance that unfortunately did not occur to God. For God; initiating civilization level 0, was sufficient, why not initiating, at least in civilization level I, or upper?

The predicament that affect us, present-day inhabitants of earth, but it will affect our children and grandchildren in the highest degree, was sent directly by God (according to the Bible), by the fact that; humans reproduce like rabbits, that way occupying the greater part of the inhabitable land, as well as, his categorical indication of our use of all natural resources, without the least care of conservation, waste, or contamination. If he knew the abuse that we would make out of the resources, at least, why did he not design them contamination free?

The *tree of right and wrong, good and evil* is evidence that; "badness" was made by God, even in paradise, it was present.

Adam and Eve were tested and failed the test, we are told, but who is to blame, us created creatures, or the designer who design us with many deficiencies.

Being that; for the Catholic church, the worst criminal, independently of the type and quantity of sins and committed crimes, can be absolved, by the simple fact of requesting forgiveness (a simple pardon me, and a few prayers, is enough), the same absurd, incomplete, inadequate and unjust learned lesson, is applied at every hierarchic level, is utilized by the church, including the Vatican. Which right now has paid millions of dollars, to compensate the incompensable. Given that raping a child, is *not compensable* and a forgiving God, with such easiness, reminds me of The Secretary of Human Rights, where he, is very worried, regarding about preserving firstly, the rights of the criminal. For the affected; *divine grace*, should be sufficient for his consolation.

EIGHT

To Big Tragedies, Big Prayers

W hy to the Catholic church (I fear that also other churches), it has not occurred to them, (or an occult purpose in not addressing the issue could exist), as the almost sure large amount of money, from the heads of the organized crime, because during all the years that I attended to mass, I never had neither Jesuits' teaching, nor in religious publications, or even in the pulpits, not ever have I listen serious advices for the youngsters to absolutely keep away from drugs or some other useful advices related to crucial predicament we are in.

In fact, it should be a commandment, that slipped God to write for Moses, but since the Catholic church, has the authority to emit, whatever comes up with, from saints' designation (taken out from the sleeve), witty remarks of miracles, appearing of virgins, criminal accomplices beatifications, etc. Well, I suggest commandment number eleven, according to its chronological order, but that should be reassigned, to number three, once it's vital importance is recognized. I admit, that I have just come up with it, but which should have been in place for at least a couple of centuries; ***"You will not try any drug never, not only even once, because they are highly addictive and because you damage your body, which you should remember, it is the body of your God's image. In like manner, this vice destroys family and society"***. In accordance, instead of excommunicating, the faithful that violate certain standards, why not excommunicate the one that turns into drugs? Yes, I know the answer; "Because he/she is a sick person", but the first time, and perhaps, even the subsequent times that is was done, a sick person was not (yet), until he/she fell into the abyss, from where almost no return exists. For this reason, at least, the excommunication for this severe behavior *should exist* for the Catholics.

But the churches, in spite of being witness of the war that the organized crime has against society (now not solely for the drugs, as such, but with extreme violence and madness), are totally mute and inactive, for them, nothing terrible occurs. Is it not this moment propitious for a fantastic example; to demonstrate *the force of praying*, if this is not it, which one can be? Why, if the church does not do it, why is it not accomplish by the believers? What if, worldwide rosaries marathons, including litanies, prayers and candles (I would not expect the inclusion of sacrifices, unless the believers would think to be absolutely necessary) where specific miracle(s) is (are) prayed for, for example: that all drugs stop instantly having his addictive force, not only that, an extreme repulsion to all that stuff could develop. Because, what we see is the complete opposite, the heads of the organized crime, continuously are finding drugs more addictive and destructive (and cheaper). The conclusion that occurs to me, is that, the aforementioned infra-humans have much better prayers, than the conventional ones, since they seem to be, much better attended. Or maybe they pray longer, or more devotedly, in more ample groups, are they more international, the drug addicts "music" (corridos), could be of God's liking, or what the hell?

Even so, would God be deaf and unfeeling to his assistant congregation to the holy mass? Why God has not given benefits for his consented creatures and mass attending, whom are at the mercy of his other malignant creatures? Would this miracle be still more impossible from conceding, than the restoration of an amputation?

Why is so immensely difficult to understand and confirm that prayers are not taken care of? Certainly, the church will not have the intention to try the above suggestion, since they would incur in a rotund proof of the falseness of praying. In principle, frankly, I do not believe that God have a minimal quota of fervent to take action, that would turn him into an indifferent God to the minorities, which the faithful do not believe. Then, why not joining together a group, the greatest possible, of one or many Catholics churches, that joined together inside or outside churches and evoke the specific prayers. This, in case that they believe that repetition is much better, like in a rosary, and repeat it as often as they believe necessary, until they become convinced, all by themselves, that prayers are not heard, not even by God.

To big catastrophes, big solutions, an acknowledged proverb reads. The terrible situation that is going on in Mexico, has forced several civic movements being the most recent, and of the most dramatic the promoted by the poet Javier Zicilia who has turned to the highest hierarchic level (terrestrial) of our country. The mafia attacks, overturns, takes revenge against the civilians, in acts of the most cruel and bestial nature. At present, the forty three disappeared students from Iguala, Guerrero, more than a month ago, plus uncountable more, and the almost daily, encounter of several graves, where the remains present a level of cruelty inconceivable, where the perpetrators have instincts far below the worst imaginable predator.

Therefore, I suggest that it is necessary to keep on climbing, in as much to the existent authorities, and the one that is pending still to recur, and the one that I invite and claim his presence, until now mute, blind and deaf entirely; the Catholic church. Right now, I believe that it is required that, either locally or still better, at corporate level, believers request that the corporate officer in charge: the CEO (Chief Executive Officer) in Rome, whose official position receives the name of Pope; to attentively coordinate as many services, meditations, prayers, oblations, and everything else, that it is consider necessary, in order that; finally God concede the miracle exposed above, and that the world gets rid of the addiction to all kinds of drugs. This miracle, if it could take place, would not free us from organized crime, due to the fact that its great organization continuously is disclosing, inventing and performing, new forms of extortion to the citizens of good behavior. Since God could be asked for the miracle, that all members of organized crime be exterminated, by some Exterminating Angel's sword (Abbadon), but I imagine that we will have to wait for the Apocalypse, it would be just too much to ask for, and too late.

If is not possible that the church takes the aforementioned action, I suggest that Catholics, independently of his church, ask for it, with very much fervor, to be able to obtain the aforementioned so important miracle. This formula that I am suggesting, is a win-win trade. That is, if the miracle comes true, Mexico (and everybody) gets rid of a great cursing (the addictive drugs) and besides, it is verified that prayers are really listened to. What amazing miracle! But if, in spite of all of the requests, it does not happen absolutely anything, the faithful (that think) will go back to give account themselves that prayers do not yield absolutely no positive result. Which also has its positive side. Now then, if neither the church, neither the faithful in independent form attempt this solution, that I am proposing, I believe that everything would indicate that nobody wants to risk to become convinced of the result that prayers grant.

Recently, I found necessary to attend to a Requiem mass, −for social ineludible motives−, which lasted two hours, because it had healings, seemed to me, that they involved practically the totality of the assistants (but me). I got stunned again when verifying the level of superstition that dominates the Catholics' brains. The priest repeated the same exact sentences, for each one that received the healing. Question: is collective healing not effective? Is it necessary to be done, in individual form? What is the reason, specifically? May God not act *in group*? Why the persons continue asking for healings, time after time, verifying in themselves, that they are not good at all? In the aforementioned mass, the priest omitted the so important prayer *Creed*, which, seems to be, next to the *Lord's Prayer* and to the *Holy Mary*, the principal Catholic prayer. This omission was due to the mentioned healings. I comment it, because it seemed very weird to me, since it is the first mass, that I remember, where the aforementioned prayer was not read. Another situation that called my attention highly was the comment of the priest, during the gospel, where he said that they commemorated this day, 500 years of the battle, (he corrected it to victory) of Lepanto's battle or something similar, where by means of the force of the rosary of all the Catholic community, it was achieved said triumph. Evidently, the priest's affirmation, referred to what I was writing in those days, in this book with respect to a generalized praying (worldwide), that according to this priest, a victory against the Turks was achieved. Why not try this force, now, against the drug cartels.

Then, I came up with the idea that the Templeton foundation, should take my suggestion, and it should show up and finance the commented experiment. What a better opportunity than this? They should not let it go. Risky, because I understand that its previous experiment, performed by Harvard's University, to carry out an investigation of heart healing on the heart surgery patients, proved to be a rotund failure. Not only that, it was counter-productive.

Why not announce this new experiment with worldwide pomp. Depending on the result, they would get established as a foundation based in the truth, or else, it would be an irrefutable proof, in order that, they close their doors, or *change business.* They could, for a change, to be dedicated to something important, like science, for example!

Let me review some of the principal miracles mentioned in the Bible:

God creates the firmament and earth, with animal and plants and man in six days.
Moses separates the waters of the sea Red
Jesus converts water into wine
Jesus resuscitates dead persons
Josue stops the movement of the sun
Etc.

In fact, *to have happened,* miracles would be true. Unfortunately, for the faithful, they are not verifiable. But, what a curious issue, over two thousand years have gone by, and no longer has anything of that stature happened? The only recent *miracles* are the appearing of one or another virgin (a unique one, is not sufficient, and giving birth without the corresponding sexual intercourse, for some dark reason, it is vital to the church). Thus a blanket with the image of the Virgin of Guadalupe, and saints' statues that bleed in some moments. What *miracles!* Yielded in our epoch, without neither the furthest transcendence, nor the furthest likeness to an event really out of the common, in comparison with the miracles above commented. What little imagination of the supposed responsible saints and church dignitaries! *Miracles*, if they could happen today, they would be able to be telecasted, on-line, to everybody, instantly. Why no longer does a single one shows up? Does God continue refusing to make himself known, now not only *to the elected tribe*, but to the entire worldwide population?

That way, as I presented the problem of drug addiction, there exist uncountable simultaneous severe problems, or worse still, predicaments for which also miracles could be requested. I would believe, that for God, it would be the same to send a miracle, or several simultaneous. Being the case, I would advise to form a group of requests and to wait to see if they take place, by means of prayers, for their celestial evaluation. It follows a list, that could conform the group of predicaments, to be miraculously solved:

Replenished, non contaminant, oil deposits
Tar sands inexistent
Exhaustion of other Natural Resources
Extinction of vegetable and animals
Global warming
Global population's absurd growth
Arsenals of weapons at several countries, especially: U.S.
Homo sapiens in danger of extinction
Etc.

Given that several of the above-mentioned points, were given by God to his supposed favorite mammal by him, explicitly, in order that, Homo sapiens could make exploitation of them, ad infinitum, perhaps, those requests by miracle, no longer can be taken into account.

In conclusion: If this is not the moment to pray, and of desperately asking for help, when will it be? To Big Tragedies, Big Prayers.

Believers of any religion, join up, show courage and guts, and ask for miracles, that is, the existence of what you believe that exist, and be prepared to get a great disappointment!

To big expectations, big frustrations! ... Or prove me wrong, and win either way.

BIBLIOGRAPHY

GOD a failed hypothesis	Victor J. Stenger
The five ages of the Universe	Fred Adams and Greg Lauglin
The God Delusion	Richard Dawkins
The Blind Watchmaker	Richard Dawkins
The Greatest Show on Earth	Richard Dawkins
God is not Great	Christofer Hitchens
The God Virus	Darrell W. Ray
Your Inner Fish	Neil Shubin
Adam's Curse	Bryan Sykes
OXYGEN The Molecule that made the World	Nick Lane
Our Final Century	Sir. Martin Rees

Printed in the United States
By Bookmasters